S.P.I.L.L
Single Parents Inspiring Love & Legacy
UPDATED

S.P.I.L.L.

Single Parents Inspiring Love and Legacy
UPDATED

A Single Parent's Guide to Intentional Parenting

LATARISS PAYNE

Thoughts & Theory Publishing, LLC

S.P.I.L.L.: Single Parents Inspiring Love & Legacy
A Single Parent's Guide to Intentional Parenting
By Latariss Payne
Thoughts & Theory Publishing, LLC

Published by Thoughts & Theory Publishing, LLC O'Fallon, MO
Copyright ©2017, ©2023 Latariss Payne
All rights reserved.

No part of this publication may be reproduced, stored in a retrieval system, or transmitted in any form or by any means, electronic, mechanical, photocopying, recording, scanning, or otherwise, except as permitted under Section 107 or 108 of the 1976 United States Copyright Act, without the prior written permission of the Publisher. Requests to the Publisher for permission should be addressed to Permissions Department, Thoughts & Theory Publishing, LLC, info@pathsetters.com.

Limit of Liability/Disclaimer of Warranty: While the publisher and author have used their best efforts in preparing this book, they make no representations or warranties with respect to the accuracy or completeness of the contents of this book and specifically disclaim any implied warranties of merchantability or fitness for a particular purpose. No warranty may be created or extended by sales representatives or written sales materials. The advice and strategies contained herein may not be suitable for your situation. You should consult with a professional where appropriate. Neither the publisher nor author shall be liable for any loss of profit or any other commercial damages, including but not limited to special, incidental, consequential, or other damages.

Editor: Katie Gearin
Book Design: Davis Creative Publishing, DavisCreativePublishing.com

Publisher's Cataloging-in-Publication
(Provided by Cassidy Cataloguing Services, Inc.)
Names: Payne, Latariss, author.
Title: S.P.I.L.L. : single parents inspiring love and legacy : a single parent's guide to intentional parenting / Latariss Payne.
Other titles: SPILL | Single parents inspiring love and legacy
Description: Updated. | O'Fallon, MO : Thoughts & Theory Publishing, LLC, [2023] | Originally published in 2017. | Includes bibliographical references.
Identifiers: ISBN: 9780999306321 (paperback) | 9780999306338 (ebook) | LCCN: 2023916273
Subjects: LCSH: Payne, Latariss--Family. | Single parents. | Parenting. | Child rearing. | Families. | BISAC: FAMILY & RELATIONSHIPS / General. | FAMILY & RELATIONSHIPS / Parenting / Single Parent. | FAMILY & RELATIONSHIPS / Parenting / General.
Classification: LCC: HQ759.915 .P39 2023 | DDC: 306.856--dc23

ACKNOWLEDGEMENTS

With special thanks:
- To my son, Cortez: Thank you for being you. I count it a privilege that God chose me to be your mother.
- To my village: Words cannot express my gratitude for the many times that each of you supported me in words and deeds in the journey of raising my son.
- To my husband, Calvin: Thank you for encouraging me to finish telling my story. Your support has been priceless.

CONTENTS

A Poem To My Son 1

Introduction 3

1. We Are Family 7
2. The Heart Of The Matter 19
3. The Best Things In Life Are Free 33
4. Let's Talk It Out 45
5. Flying Solo 59
6. Count The Cost 71
7. Do As I Say, Not As I Do 85
8. It's Not About Me 95
9. Life Happens 107

Notes 119

A POEM TO MY SON

Biggest Fan

    I still look in on you when you are asleep and smile because you are mine
    I pulled myself up so that through me you could see you how far you could climb
    At times, I've cried myself to sleep at night and worried if I was enough
    And with a blink of an eye, I saw myself carrying us through all kinds of stuff.
    It's an amusement park life that we live minus the tea cup rides
    There have been twist and turns; ups and downs but if I put all those things aside
    I've been your mom, your teacher, your counselor, your nurse, your coach, your mentor, and your friend
    Even when you fall short, in my heart, I am secretly holding up a card that has a perfect score of ten.
    In times of struggle I've admired your humility and your determination to fight through
    Those moments are the most rewarding because I see that I've done some things right with you
    I'm filled with the love and joy of raising a boy who has become an amazing young man
    I held you in my arms so long ago and now I'm learning to let go.
    Love Always…Your Biggest Fan

Introduction

"Life is like a box of chocolates."
– Forrest Gump

It was Valentine's Day, and instead of celebrating love and romance, I sat in a courtroom staring at the judge while he asked if I wanted to return to my maiden name. It was the final question I faced before my marriage ended. The circumstances that brought me to that place crashed down and left me feeling a sense of utter disappointment and failure. My brain was stuck on the question about my maiden name like I was a contestant on Jeopardy, and the "Think!" theme was about to stop. After I answered, my focus quickly shifted, and my mind was fixated on my son. There were many reflections on the emotional impact that divorce would have on him before that day. I walked out of that court building, no longer married but still the mother of a six-year-old little boy. His name is Cortez, and he was at school like it was a normal day. He didn't have a clue as to what was going on that morning. Becoming a single parent wasn't a predictable process; it was like the great philosopher Forrest Gump said, "a box of chocolates."[1] I didn't know what I was getting. There was no preparation to deal with the emotional, financial, and social responsibilities of parenting alone. Being a single parent has been amazing, hard, delightful, scary, rewarding, costly, phenomenal, and ordinary. Whether you are pregnant and about to become a single parent or your children are in high school, ready to chart their path in life, this book is for you and about you.

Divorce was new for me, but I wasn't completely unfamiliar with the life of a single parent. My mother and grandmother raised me, and not having my father in my life was unpleasant. I knew from personal experience that, for my son's sake, sinking was not an option, so I learned how to swim. I discovered how to tread water in the shallow pool of single parenting and, eventually, how to swing my arms and kick my feet.

When my son's father abandoned him, it was like someone pushed me into deep waters without a life jacket. However, instead of drowning, I grabbed the nearest board and learned to ride the waves. My most significant decision was to try to understand and learn what my son deserved and needed from me in his father's absence. I was determined to raise my son to be a good, productive, healthy kid who would eventually become a caring, responsible, and honorable young man. Along the way, I've faced the undercurrents and extreme waves of being a single parent.

I've observed statistics about children raised in single-parent homes and decided my son wouldn't be just a statistic. I wanted to understand ways to minimize his risk of falling into specific patterns and behaviors. There are no absolutes in parenting, but there is evidence that how you raise your children can bring about a profound change for your family. I want to help other single parents experience the joy of raising their children with family values that will lift and carry them out of the isolation and the stigma stamped on children raised in single-parent homes.

Hindsight is always 20/20, but I am not just looking back at the lessons I've learned. I'm looking forward to my son's future. My testimony is not that my son is an adult and he turned out great. My story is that my journey was intentional and purposeful while raising him.

By the time you finish this book, I hope that you will begin to understand that you must confront some trials that are unique to single parents. I am the product of a single-parent home. While writing this book, I was still on the front line and in the trenches raising my son. I can speak to the emotional, financial, physical, social, and spiritual aspects of being a single parent.

This is by no means the ultimate book of single parenting or a version of single parenting for dummies, but if I could teach *Single Parenting 101*, specific topics would be part of my curriculum. In the following chapters, I will share tips to help you as you face economic disparity, discipline issues, emotional concerns, and decision fatigue. These topics are essential for all parents and can be difficult to nurture, but it can be even more challenging when one individual is trying to cover all the bases.

In the documentary "The Family Project," psychologist Dr. John Townsend stated, "Society is built on family. Family is a foundational building block of what creates a good society. If we don't put the energy we need into building healthy, strong, loving, productive families, society is in trouble. Your society is no better than your family structures."[2] Dr. Townsend's statement underscores one of the purposes of this book. Having a father and mother in the home isn't always an end-all solution, but it is rewarding when children have two parents devoted to their marriage and family.

I couldn't give my son the home I desired where his father and I would love and raise him, but I could give him the gift of a loving home with the same guiding principles and values that help contribute to his well-being and future. I can share a legacy of love with my son that he can treasure. A legacy that brings hope to his life and others. Take this journey with me to discover how you can raise your children and nurture your family in a way that will affect future generations. Get comfortable; we've got a lot to chat about.

CHAPTER ONE

We Are Family

"I sustain myself with the love of family."
— Maya Angelou

Kids are some of the most honest people around. They tell it like it is and don't leave much room for anything else. There's usually no need for interpretation, conjecture, or translation. When my son Cortez was younger, he would interrupt me when I would reference us as a family and say, "We are not a family because there is no dad here with us."

How is that for telling it like it is? He was right. His dad wasn't in our home with us anymore, but this remarkable kid gave me his definition of family. Over the next several years, I would find myself doing a balancing act of validating my son's incredible definition that a family is a father, mother, and children while uplifting our single-parent family, esteeming it, and declaring that we were an extraordinary family too.

Changing Families

Cortez's elementary school offered several youth counseling programs. I enrolled him in one called the "Changing Families." This program consisted of group counseling sessions for children mostly from single-parent homes. Single-parent families can develop from any number of life situations. Without question, the death of a spouse is one of the most difficult and grievous situations. I cannot imagine coping with the loss of a husband or wife and adjusting to parenting alone. Some children are cared for by an amazing single parent who is not their birth parent. I admire a family member, adoptive parent, or foster parent who chooses to love and raise children abandoned by one or both parents or who has lost both parents due to death.

My single parenting was fragmented. I spent much of his life as a single mom due to divorce and his earlier years as an unwed, single mother. Divorce can be a destructive life situation for children. No matter how amicable, a family is permanently torn apart, which can have a lasting impact. The children in the counseling sessions fell into these life circumstances.

I received a call one day from the counselor asking if I had read Cortez's journal from the counseling sessions.

"Yes, I have."

"How accurate are his accounts of his home life and relationship with his father?"

"Extremely accurate. Why do you ask?"

"I've never seen a seven-year-old be so descriptive of his feelings. Cortez has shown deep sadness, sometimes anger, and other times he seems isolated in the sessions with the other students. He is not lashing out at any of them, but I found he has the gift of expressing those same emotions in his journals."

We talked in depth about specific things that Cortez shared, but the real takeaway was that my experience with him at home focused heavily on the sadness and disappointment he felt about his dad not consistently being in his life. Early on, those feelings were usually triggered by an expectation of his father that wasn't met. As he got older, he began to express his pain and confusion by being indifferent and irritable. Those changes were subtle at home but very evident through situations at school. As a parent, it isn't easy to recognize regular growing pains instead of outward displays of emotional pain.

My awareness of Cortez's emotional struggles came from studying him over the years. I guess, in layperson's terms, it came from knowing my kid. At different phases of his life, his security of what he believed about family changed. Like all of us, children go through life learning how to process hurt and will protect themselves in different ways. My responses changed over time based on his level of maturity, but my love for him, sense of stability, and attentiveness were the best support I could give him.

Enrolling Cortez in the Changing Families Counseling Program was a conscious decision to give him a safe place to talk about his feelings, and he could see that he wasn't the only kid whose parents were divorced. Family is the strongest influence in a child's environment, and it is a foundation that shapes their view of the rest of the world. It is important not to ignore or exaggerate the significance of being raised by two parents. Regardless of the family structure, two-parent and single-parent families should have a well-balanced perspective of the purpose and benefit of parenting well.

What is Family

What does family mean to people anymore? The definition of family can be broad in context, but I want to talk about family from the perspective of parents and their children. Extended family and close friends, who are like family, are essential in child-rearing, and I will talk about them later when we look at having a sound support system.

The 1913 version of the Webster dictionary defines family as "The group comprising of a husband and wife and their dependent children, constituting a fundamental unit in the organization of society."[1] *Dictionary.com* updated and broadened the definition of family in 2016, by defining it as, "A basic social unit consisting of parents and their children, considered as a group, whether dwelling together or not, or a social unit consisting of one or more adults together with the children they care for."[2]

The 1913 definition of the family suggests that a traditional or nuclear family is a two-parent home. More and more, there are many non-traditional family structures as defined by today's standards. Family can mean many things to different people and cultures, but how strong of an argument can be made against the fact that children benefit significantly from having the love and influence of both a father and a mother as expressed in the traditional sense? I'm not saying that two-parent homes are perfect. There are harmful circumstances that can exist across any family structure. If presented in any home, physical abuse, sexual abuse, drug abuse, neglect, and an array of other problems are detrimental to the welfare of a child. The best interest of any child is to have a loving home, and I passionately believe that the single-family structure can provide a loving environment.

Let's return to Cortez's remark: "We are not a family because there is no dad here with us." Hearing my son make such a bold statement fascinated me because he held firm to his conviction. To him, family was synonymous with marriage. His comment also made me sad. I felt sorrow and guilt because the emotional consequences of divorce began to rear its ugly head. At a very young age, Cortez questioned if his father loved him. I didn't know if my answers were enough to satisfy him because the answers I got when I was a kid never satisfied me. Cortez's dad and I separated when he was five years old. His dad started as an every-other-weekend dad. Over a short time, he slowly began to drop out of his life and disappeared entirely for several years. Our divorce and his dad's subsequent decision to abandon him set the stage for what I would consider my greatest battle as a parent, which was protecting Cortez's self-worth.

Every child is different, but children are hard-wired to desire the love of a father and a mother. Have you ever considered that no matter how society attempts to define marriage, human life begins with the fertilization of the sperm of a man and the egg of a woman? That is by design and can't be changed by science or society. Ideally, an intimate relationship and connection between a husband and a wife should be nurtured and passed on as they begin raising children. A void will exist when one or both parents are missing.

Single-parent families may not fall into the definition of the traditional family, and that is okay. Changing the definition of the traditional family is like changing the definition of baseball. Baseball is only baseball if you have a bat and a ball. You are playing something else if you do not have a bat. If one parent is missing, you have something else. Even with changes to our circumstances, such as being in a single-parent or blended family, the word "family" can remain intact.

Single parents can live with the principles and values represented in the original definitions of family, regardless of the attitudes and opinions of our culture. The design for the family can be honored without compromising the definition, even if we are flying solo as parents. In my loudest shout, I am screaming to all single parents: "WE ARE FAMILY."

My Greatest Fear

If you asked anyone that I grew up around, both adults and kids my age, I would have been voted the least likely to be a good mother. Not because I didn't like or want children, I just didn't display any signs of being maternal. I was a tomboy, loved to play basketball, and didn't start wearing makeup until my late 20s. In other words, I was a late bloomer when it came to tapping into my femininity. I played with dolls and jumped rope like other little girls, but I preferred to roughhouse with the boys if given a choice. I favored Ken over Barbie, hot wheels over easy bake ovens, and I was better than most boys at video games. I did not fit the prototype of a little girl destined for motherhood greatness. I had a less-than-stellar maternal resume; no real indication that I had any motherly instincts. I never wanted to bring a child into the world to have him repeat my awful experience of growing up without a father, but my life changed forever when I found out I was pregnant with my son.

After the third pregnancy test, I gradually stepped backward until my back was against my bathroom wall. I slid down the wall in disbelief that I was pregnant. I sat on the floor with tears streaming down my face. The only thought running through my mind was, "This can't be happening to me, not right now." Just one month earlier, I decided I wanted to leave the emotionally abusive relationship I had been in for many years.

As I sat there crying in complete and utter disappointment with myself, I touched my stomach with both hands and the reality that a little person was inside me aroused a deep appreciation for life. I gracefully got up off the floor and took a deep breath. With my head down and my hands gripping the corner of the sink, I began to replay all the emotions I felt in my life up until that moment. I hated myself, and I hated my life. I was embarrassed, ashamed, and frustrated with my decisions in that relationship. I had allowed a man to drain me and strip me of my identity and self-worth. I had spiraled into a deep, dark depression and felt like I was about to fall off a cliff into a pit of despair and hopelessness. Yet, in the muddiness of those emotions, there was a clear and undeniable acceptance of my situation. With dried tear stains on my face, I found a reason to crack a smile, then a little grin that turned into a wide, deep, dimple smile. I became keenly aware that life was no longer just about me. The baby inside of me was counting on me. I didn't have a plan, but I knew one thing for sure; I wanted my baby, and there was no other decision to be made even though he was conceived in an unfavorable situation. I married my son's father when he was two years old, and we divorced a few years later.

This is how I became a single mother again. I asked my son for his blessing to share this story with you. As I read it to him, I was overwhelmed with emotion and cried. I thought back to my pregnancy and fear of becoming a mother. I was twenty-five years old, with a college degree and a decent job. While I was very independent, I was still terrified to think of having the responsibility of caring for another life.

I didn't wear being a single parent as a badge of honor, nor did I wear it as a symbol of disgrace. I acknowledge that I was responsible for preparing my son to enter this world and become a man. Though he will make his own decisions, I owed him my love, nurturing, discipline, and guidance so that he would have a good foundation for building his own life. I didn't take that commitment lightly.

A lot of outside forces will impact a child's perceptions of family. You should be the most important person in their lives and be responsible for teaching them family values that will guide their future. You are capable of being an amazing parent and provider for your children. By provider, I don't just mean financially. I mean being the sole or primary source for meeting your children's varying needs. It's not easy to bear such a significant responsibility, but you can impact your children's tomorrow by deliberately parenting well today.

~SINGLE PARENT 101~
Strengthening Your Family

- *What principles and values do you want to establish in your home?*

    I became a Christian when I was pregnant with my son. Biblical principles became the foundation for our home. I taught him universal values, such as being kind, honest, and respectful. The key was teaching him at an early age and enforcing those ideals as he continued to mature.

- *How can you show your children that they are important to you?*

    Combining words and actions has allowed me to express my love for my son. Saying I love you isn't enough. I've always attended important events for him, but I've also found that giving him my undivided attention makes him feel important.

- *What family traditions can you create to build a special connection with your children?*

    Taking family vacations creates beautiful memories. You can also do things that are simple and free. Find television shows or games you like and pick nights to spend quality time together. This is priceless when everyone's schedules are hectic.

- *Do you have age-appropriate conversations about significant changes that will affect your family?*

    Cortez was in the 5th grade when I purchased our first home. He was very nervous about attending a new school and making new friends. I talked to him early and often to reassure him. It didn't completely remove his anxiety, but I believe he had more confidence to face the changes.

CHAPTER TWO

The Heart of the Matter

"All the knowledge I possess everyone else can acquire, but my heart is all my own."
— Johann Wolfgang von Goethe

In 2014, there was a standing ovation as the camera spanned across the room while Kevin Durant wrapped up his Most Valuable Player (MVP) speech. It was hard to believe that some people were not a little choked up as Kevin humbly said to his mother, "You are the real MVP."[1] This statement came after he discussed a list of sacrifices she made as a single mother raising him and his brother. During one of the most important days of his life, Kevin acknowledged his mother and the sacrifices she made so that he had a chance to make something of his life. His mother could only sit with tears of joy rolling down her face as she watched the MVP of the National Basketball Association remember the love he received and felt during the tough times of his upbringing. I had the pleasure of meeting Wanda Durant, Kevin's mother, and I was inspired to hear the story of a mother raising boys and overcoming the many obstacles that can exist when there are no silver spoons in sight.

Listening to Wanda Durant reminded me of a statement I once heard, "I don't know of anyone who has a harder place in life than the single mother. The single mother has to be the soft and the hard. She has to be the kind and the firm and everything else in the home."[2]

Comments like this one and Kevin Durant's heartfelt devotion toward his mother hit close to home and tugged deeply at my heart. My personal family experiences have their strongest roots in the single-family structure. Until I was almost 30 years old, I had three generations of women who raised me and influenced my life. My great-grandmother, grandmother, and mother were the strongest women I have ever known. While all of them were married at one time or another, much of my life with them was while they were single mothers. Each of them, in their way, instilled characteristics and qualities that I hold dear to my heart. They taught me how to have the "do whatever it takes" drive I have today. As I have gotten older, I suspect their "do whatever it takes" attitude was triggered because there simply wasn't anyone else to do what needed to be done to care for our family.

In my early childhood, fatherless homes were very typical. I knew my father's identity, but he was never involved in my life. I've had good and bad experiences as a child raised by a single parent. My father's absence made me feel unwanted and unloved. I stuffed those feelings, and they weighed me down like an oversized suitcase. While raising my son, I have faced the struggles of living through many difficult situations, such as the financial strain of one income not being enough. Through these struggles, I have found another perspective that made me think differently about being a single parent.

Let's face it; it's tough no matter how you got here. A better place for me isn't wishing I had help raising my son or having more money. The better place is knowing that no matter what comes or what goes, I did my best to improve my life and provide a loving home for my son. I know the heart of a child raised by a single parent, and I deeply understand the heart of a single parent raising a child. When I discovered the importance and benefits of being raised by a father and a mother, I embraced stepping outside my own experience. I opened myself up to looking for opportunities to fill the void my son was experiencing.

The Facts Still Remain

Being a single parent isn't the road less traveled. It is a path traveled by many. According to the U.S. Census Bureau, out of about 12 million single-parent families in 2016, more than 83% were headed by single mothers and over 17% by single fathers.[3] The National Principals Association Report on the State of High Schools shows that 70% of all high school dropouts are teens from single-parent homes.[4] The Single Parent Success Foundation cites that more than half of all youths incarcerated in the U.S. lived in one-parent families as a child.[5]

Those numbers are staggering. I'm a facts kind of girl, so I like statistics. I like to analyze things, and I do mean all kinds of stuff. It is one of my strong suits but can also be an Achilles heel if not careful. I can appreciate data and probabilities until they are leaned on too much and allowed to give a wrong perspective. It's true that numbers don't lie, but they don't always tell the whole story, either.

The old "do the math" saying is all about logic, another of my favorite topics. When people say do the math, they mean "the conclusion or the answer is pretty obvious if you add it all up or look at the facts." Based on the numbers, society has much to say about children who grow up in single-parent homes compared to two-parent homes.

Seeing negative statistics about children who grow up in single-parent homes are tough. There is no way to know that coming from a single-parent home is the only driving force behind the numbers. Children who come from loving two-parent homes can make bad choices and fall into devastating situations as well. Successful parenting isn't defined by how your children turn out. It is defined by how you care for them along the way.

Take a moment and think about your life. Like me, you are flawed, tired, and probably made a few mistakes. Nonetheless, you are still here, and despite the statistics, even if your children are preparing to leave home, there are still so many opportunities to help them mature and be encouraged about their future. You don't lose your children when they leave home, but the relationship changes. While they still need your guiding hand, you can raise your boys and teach them to be honorable men who desire to be strong husbands and good fathers. You can nurture your girls and teach them to be virtuous women who desire to be excellent wives and loving mothers. You can encourage and support others to help build strong families that can tell other stories. You can tell stories of the other side of those horrible statistics. I'm a single parent, but I wrote this book to help other single parents. I had to raise my son alone, but I returned to school and got a Master's Degree. It has been an uphill battle, but I am a business owner. I have many "buts" in my life, and I bet you do too.

Children with both parents in the home have two people to depend on and rely on, but in your home, you are the Tower of Pisa. You might be leaning to the side and worn down, but you are still standing and strong enough to withstand the trials and tribulations of parenting by yourself. You may have to make hard decisions that push you into your "but" moment. Your children are worth every "but" moment you can create for them. You become the best parent you can be by making one good decision at a time.

Fighting Against the Odds

I'm not a big fan of movie remakes, and a horrible rendition makes me appreciate the creativity of the original. There simply cannot be a successful replacement for Mr. Miagi and Daniel from the 1984 film *The Karate Kid*. There is no movie watcher alive who has seen *The Karate

Kid and doesn't go away with several messages about overcoming adversity or who doesn't leave without a sense of admiration for the bond shared between a student and his mentor. The relationship between Mr. Miagi and Daniel left us waxing on and off and feeling inspired by Mr. Miagi's many words of wisdom. Most people would easily give *The Karate Kid* a 4 out of 5 stars for this riveting story about victory and the fight of the underdog.

I give it a 5 out of 5 because there is an indirect but powerful message within the plot of *The Karate Kid* that tells another fascinating story. It is Lucille's story. I'm sure I've left you scratching your head and asking, "Who the heck is Lucille?" Lucille is Daniel's mother.

Lucille is a single mom raising her teenage son, Daniel, who is an only child. The movie begins with Lucille packing her and Daniel into a beat-up station wagon, heading across the country over 2,700 miles from Newark, New Jersey, to Los Angeles, California, to start a new job in hopes of giving them a new start. The movie ends with her running out to Daniel, who can barely stand because of an injury to his leg. He is then lifted triumphantly in the air holding a karate trophy after winning a grueling tournament against his nemesis, who tormented him throughout the movie. Planted in this storyline is a narrative of Lucille's fight for her son. I hope that I've given you just enough juicy details to have you go and watch *The Karate Kid* for the first time or to watch it again if you haven't seen it in years so that you can look for these subtle moments of single mom greatness:[6]

- **Lucille's move from New Jersey to California** – *Sometimes, you have to remove yourself and your children from situations or locations that are harmful or don't allow you to prosper.*
- **Lucille's attentiveness to Daniel's struggles** – *You must be sensitive to your children's needs. They demonstrate verbal and non-verbal cues, and you have to lean in with them and learn how to connect with them so that they know it is safe to come to you.*
- **Lucille's support of Daniel's dreams** – *Much like Wanda Durant, Lucille's love and support elevated her son's belief in himself that he could accomplish his dream of competing in the karate tournament.*
- **Lucille's acceptance of help** – *Lucille couldn't afford to pay Mr. Miagi, but she humbled herself and accepted a man's offer to help her son. She was working to better their situation but wasn't ashamed that they didn't have much money or an active male role model in her son's life.*

Lucille's sacrifices for Daniel are the decisions that all parents will face when the other parent is absent. These are decisions that I've had to make for my son. Your family might go through the same struggles, and you may have to tackle issues alone, but I'm here to tell you that you should not be without hope. No matter what stage or circumstance you are in, you can consciously decide right now to grab hold of your family and fight for yourself and your children's future.

Lucille left New Jersey to make a better life for her son. I can identify with that decision. Until the age of thirteen, I lived in East Saint Louis, Illinois. Google it, and you will find a YouTube video that describes the city as having the strangest and most abandoned downtown in America. Growing up, we were lower-middle class and living in a neighborhood that was becoming destitute. I had my share of government cheese and didn't see anything wrong with using food stamps to buy snacks. I saw violence committed up close and saw first-hand what drug addiction can do to a family. My mother moved my older brother and me to the city of Berkeley, which at the time, was a nice suburb outside of the city of St. Louis, Missouri. Before the move, single mothers made up a large part of our old neighborhood. My father was non-existent, and my brother's father died when he was four. My mother worked hard to put herself through nursing school, and the struggle was real for my grandmother, who raised her eight children and some of her grandchildren, including me. Being uprooted as a teenager was hard, and my mother didn't do a great job preparing me or helping me through it, but I can honestly say it was a great decision.

Although I grew up with examples of strong women all around me, I began to question the effects of having a father and a mother in the home when I was in high school. After moving to a new state and attending a new high school, I noticed that many of my friends had both parents or at least one parent and a step-parent in the home. My mother had just married then, but my stepfather wasn't consistently caring for his children. Exposure to my friend's two-parent households was an eye-opening experience because it helped me see relationships, family, and, specifically, the need for fathers differently.

Becoming More than Enough

Sacrifices come in all sizes and shapes. I remember starting a new job and having no sick time to call off work. My son was sick, and I had been up throughout the night with him. After emptying out all he had eaten the night before and then some, he cuddled up next to me and was sound asleep. Looking at him sleep, I knew he felt safe and didn't have a care in the world. As I lay there trying to figure out my options, I'm not sure what bothered me more, not having the sick time, not having someone I could call on short notice, or the negative impression I would leave on a new manager. The truth is that no matter what was going on in my head, there was no conflict in my heart. My heart was solely concerned about the health of my son, and caring for him overrode any feelings of worry about anything else.

You've been there. You know the feelings of being sleep deprived and staying home to tend to your sick child. You know the courage to put family first and what it means to put your children's needs before yours. Most parents will identify with many of the situations I am sharing throughout this book, but only single parents can fully comprehend what it feels like to have the eyes of a child look to them and them alone, to meet all their needs.

Cortez turned sixteen while I was writing this book, and my fight for him is no different from Lucille's or Wanda's fight. I remember the look in his eyes when he looked to me and me alone for everything he needed. We were on this journey together. We learned to embrace and appreciate our single-parent family structure. Regardless of the bumps along the way or the desire to have something different, I returned to that moment on my bathroom floor, rubbing my stomach, and embracing that this life is not just about me. You can be your children's MVP and their biggest fan. You can be in their corner, fight against the odds, and overcome the adversities of parenting alone.

What is fighting against the odds? Do you remember the numbers? You are fighting against financial pressures, isolation, decision pressure, guilt, and being plain old worn out. You fight against the odds one decision at a time. Even the most minor decisions can instill a sense of family in your children and make all the difference in your home.

I am more Diana Prince than I am anyone else. Before the 2017 movie, if you were not a fan, like me, you may have scratched your head, asking, "Who the heck is Diana Prince?" Everyone knows Clark Kent is Super Man's alias, and Bruce Wayne is Batman's alias, but I didn't know much about Diana Prince, who is Wonder Woman's alter ego. Most women like to identify with Super Girl, and even if you go with Wonder Woman, you've got me beat. On my best day, I don't wear an "S" on my chest with a cape, and I surely don't sport a strapless swimsuit with boots. Now Diana Prince, on the other hand, I can relate to her.

Her comic book character was complex and evolved over the years, from having a career as an Army nurse to a military intelligence officer and businesswoman while caring enough to still want to save the world.

My strongest moments come from being the everyday alter ego who wears many hats, not the version of Wonder Woman who can do it all. It was when I did everyday life with my son that I saw how strong I was. Over the years, if I allowed them to, feelings of inadequacy would have eaten me alive. Fears of failure would have swallowed me whole. Worries about not being enough would have chewed me up and spit me out. I have so many "but" moments that I can't count all of them.

If you are parenting alone, you are the only one your children look to for everything they need. Being "everything" in the home means the whole shebang. However you say it, you are the most important person in your children's lives, and that is not an easy hat to wear. You are a single mother or single father carrying the entire load. Imagine that I am giving you a hug or a fist bump and let that speak to your heart right now because I am saying, "You are good enough." If nobody ever says it, I'm telling you that the decision to raise your children instead of aborting, abandoning, or making someone else responsible for caring for them speaks very loudly. We are family, and you are more than enough.

~SINGLE PARENT 101~
Understanding Your Heart

- *Can you pinpoint areas in parenting that you struggle with the most?*

    When you focus on your weaknesses more than you do your strengths, it makes you feel inadequate overall. Getting help in a particular area may be as simple as getting a book on the subject and putting one of the recommendations into practice.

- *Are you able to isolate decisions in your past that contribute to your thoughts about yourself?*

    The way that you were raised influences how you raise your children. No parent gets everything right. For example, if your parent(s) was harsh and crushed your self-esteem, don't repeat those types of patterns of behavior with your children.

- *Do you have a close relative or friend you can confide in about your struggles?*

    Your village should have people to help with child-rearing, but it should also include having someone for you to talk with. Isolation can cause depression. Stay connected with others or find a support group.

- *What tugs at your heart as a single parent?*

    As a mother raising a son, I wanted to understand and help him get through some developmental milestones. I have a circle of trustworthy men looking out for my son, but there are great online resources and books available that can help with raising children of the opposite gender.

CHAPTER THREE

The Best Things in Life are Free

"Why is there so much month left at the end of the money."
– John Barrymore

The best things in life are free is a beautiful and inspirational proverb. Unfortunately, we need more than the beautiful freebies of love, peace, and joy to survive. While you certainly need those things, the fundamental things you provide for your children, such as nourishment, shelter, and clothes, cost money. Financial pressure is a big problem that many face daily. I've been on both ends of the spectrum. I've seen hard times and times of more than enough. Without any child support, I have cared for my son on my income for most of his life. When I divorced, my world was turned upside down, and I had to start over…literally. I lived with a good friend and her family, which allowed me to rebound emotionally and financially. My choice was a humbling experience, and I was very fortunate to have that option. Asking for help was very difficult, but eventually, I realized it wasn't a sign of weakness.

I don't despise the days of humble beginnings or other seasons of financial struggle. I received assistance through the Special Supplemental Nutrition Program called WIC (Women, Infants, and Children) when Cortez was born. When you face financial difficulties, don't have enough money to pay bills, and can't give your children the things they need, it is scary and can cause significant stress. It has been many years since I lived with my friend. I faced those obstacles head-on, but I didn't give up. It wasn't smooth sailing for me to get to that place, but having a financial plan along the way gave me the focus to better my situation. A financial plan is not just for people who make a certain amount of money. It's for anyone who wants to see the big picture and set short-term and long-term goals for their family to be able to map out a way to change their financial situation.

Other financial options like government assistance programs get a bad rap because many people abuse the system, but they are meant to be temporary. I needed help from a friend. Help may come from a housing, food, or medical assistance program. It may need to come from family, friends, or other community assistance. Working more than one job is a huge sacrifice as well. My heart goes out to any parent who must work two or more jobs to care for their children. How do you choose between being present or putting food on the table and clothes on their back? That is a tough situation, and it is an unfair fight for those who are doing their best to care for their children. The best you can do is make every moment count!

The Forest for the Trees

Approximately 60% of U.S. children living in mother-only families are impoverished, compared with only 11% of two-parent families.[1] The poverty rate is even higher in African-American single-parent families, where two out of every three children are poor.[1] Poverty is also linked with single fatherhood: more than one-third (36%) of fathers living at or below the poverty line are single parents.[3] When you can't financially provide for your family and are faced with the possibility of being homeless, life looks different than just struggling to pay a bill every month.

Single parents fall into a wide range of financial circumstances. You may never know what it feels like not to know where your children's next meal is coming from. If that's you, be grateful and find contentment in your situation. If you are struggling, and that is your reality, there is always hope. When given the testimony of others who have overcome what you are battling, you must know that your current situation doesn't have to be your destiny or the legacy you leave for your children.

Sometimes you can't see the forest for the trees. You are so entrenched in the day-to-day of your challenges that you don't stop to confront the how or the why. Sometimes, the *how* and *why* don't matter, and you need to push forward. But if you are stuck in a cycle of financial struggles or have never lived with financial peace, then pushing forward will be in vain. Your perspective about your life shapes the way you live your life. Your lifestyle and financial condition will not change if you don't change how you think. Perhaps financial hardship is all you have ever known and seen. Maybe your situation came about through one decision that spiraled out of control, and you have been unable to bounce back, or you are simply encountering a temporary setback. Wealth doesn't give you security, but it does give you the means to meet essential needs for you and your children, and it positions you to do good by giving to others in need.

Chris Gardner, portrayed in the movie, *The Pursuit of Happyness*, is a father, an ambitious businessman, and a multi-millionaire, but his life wasn't always a glowing portrait of stability.

In an article by Belinda Elliott on CBN, she tells the story of Chris when he was in his late 20s and found himself homeless on the streets of San Francisco with his infant son. The father and son were forced to move from place to place, seeking shelter wherever they could. They spent many nights in a church-operated homeless shelter, but when the shelter was full, Gardner and his son found refuge elsewhere, including in a subway bathroom. Gardner's luck changed when he applied for an internship with a stock brokerage firm. He secured a spot in the Dean Witter Reynolds training program. Gardner knew nothing about the business, but he was determined to do whatever it took to succeed and impress his employer. His hard work at the brokerage firm paid off. He was the only trainee in the program to be offered a job with the company. He rose through the ranks, eventually accepted a job at another firm, and later started his firm, Gardner Rich & Co., in Chicago.

Gardner said his top priority was to be a good father to his son. Gardner never knew his birth father and his stepdad was unkind. Now a multi-millionaire, Gardner looks back on those days and remembers the pain he suffered. He is thankful that he now has the opportunity to reach out to others facing the same struggles. Speaking around the country, he meets single fathers who are struggling but who desire to make a better life for their kids.

Chris has a fantastic testimony and made a profound statement about his mother. "I chose to embrace the spirit of my mother," Gardner said, "who thought she had too many of her own dreams denied, deferred, and destroyed, she still instilled in me her child, that I could have dreams, and that I did have a responsibility and the power."[3] Chris' testimony is uplifting and encouraging. When there is no other parent to help carry the burden, it can be a disheartening situation. We take for granted the emotional support from a spouse or significant other during a financial crisis. The average person, married or single, can experience heaviness or deep depression during this time. It may be processed internally, displayed outwardly through negative actions, or a person can be in denial. The hope that things will turn around, the possibility that someone might be able to help you, the fear of not being able to feed your children, or the dreaded feelings of failure can take you on a roller coaster ride that is sure to leave you dizzy and sick when you get off.

"New normal" is the term given when conditions in life that were previously thought of as irregular become commonplace. I want you to have confidence that your current situation does not have to be your new normal. If all you've been exposed to is a world of never having enough to meet your family's essential needs, shift your thinking to the possibility that there are solutions to help you better your situation.

I'm talking to a single mom who lives in low-income housing because she is on welfare. I'm speaking to a single dad whose wife left him, and he is trying to raise his children on one income. This is for those of you who have lost a spouse, are left with a pile of debt, and can't see a way out. This is for anybody who has poorly managed their finances and doesn't know how to get back on track.

Today is now. You can't change yesterday, but you can alter your family's future by making good choices today. The better choice can be just thinking differently and having hope. You can start there and begin to act. Be intentional about finding available resources, organizations, programs, and charities to give financial assistance. Getting child support from the other parent is the best help you can ask for, but if you are not getting that type of support, seek other options. For many, it may take returning to school to get your high school diploma or further your education to find a new job or a better position. For others, it will mean asking for help with childcare so that you can get a job or take on a part-time job. If you have a habit of being financially irresponsible, don't let your children continue to suffer through your bad decision-making. Make a conscious choice to stop doing that for their sake. None of us are perfect. Second chances and sometimes third or fourth chances are a reality that you must give yourself to overcome the challenges of caring for your children when you are the only one providing for their well-being.

Wisdom in the Pastures

Perhaps you haven't had adversity in finances while parenting your children alone. You aren't in the forest and can see clear across the green pastures. You have either been very comfortable, or maybe you are well off financially. There is nothing wrong with that. There are valuable lessons to learn in any situation, and I wouldn't wish poverty on anyone.

Lacking money is stressful, but that's not the only financial pressure to contend with. It's more prevalent when the parents are divorced, but overcompensating for an absent or negligent parent can also be harmful. It can occur when co-parenting and you don't spend enough time with your kids. Trying too hard to please your children with things and stuff is triggered by guilt. A continuous YES to their wants and desires will hurt you financially and give them the power to manipulate you. Lavishing them with material things will not show them how to cope in the real world when the word NO will be a common occurrence. It hurts to see your children in pain, disappointed, and upset, and you want to make things better. Paying for their silence or loyalty is not the answer. Seeing your children smile instead of throwing a tantrum or having ungrateful attitudes is nice, but the reality is that they will do those things whenever they don't get their way. At any age, children need to learn how to handle disappointment, respond appropriately, and be responsible for their actions.

Cortez is my only child. Being a single parent of an only child has its own set of challenges. There was no other sibling to play with, talk to, lean on, learn with, grow with, and even fight with. While he has never competed for my love, attention, time, or money, there were times when I still felt like I wasn't doing enough. I worked full-time; he was an only child, and not having his dad around seemed like a lot for a kid to handle. The awareness that he didn't need me to overcompensate came very innocently.

It was our first Christmas after his dad and I separated. We were living with my friend, and my financial situation was horrible. I was in bankruptcy, I had been forced out of our home, and I was trying to adjust to the changes. Dealing with the emotional and financial fallout was overwhelming. Yet, I had this little bright-eyed kid I wanted to smother with love and give whatever gifts I could muster up for him on Christmas day.

He was a huge wrestling fan, so I got him this ultimate deluxe wrestling ring and a few other gifts. Other presents from family and friends made a difference for him that year. I was super excited because I knew he would love the new John Cena action figure and the wrestling ring. This ring had the cage, the commentator table, and cool stickers.

As he ripped the wrapping paper open, Cortez's face lit up when he saw the box with the wrestling ring. As the morning went on, I noticed he never asked me to put the ring together. I found him blissfully playing with the action figures on the wrestling ring box. He played with the box more than the actual ring for weeks. The box was colorful, and on the back, it had an image of the ring and pictures of other wrestlers.

I learned it didn't take spending much money to make him happy. As he got older, I talked with him and prepared him for tough financial times. He has shown a deeper level of understanding than I could have ever imagined and a humble appreciation for the gifts he receives for his birthday and other moments of celebration. I'm not saying he hasn't been disappointed or self-centered at times, but his responses have been more compassionate and gracious than selfish and vain. There are special times when I splurge a bit, like a milestone birthday, which has nothing to do with overcompensating. If I'm financially able to do it, I believe in creating exceptional memories for significant moments in life.

Hard circumstances in life have a way of rocking the boat in many areas of your life, but love conquers all and covers a multitude of bad deeds. This includes bad deeds someone else did to you by leaving you or abandoning your children. Love also triumphs over your poor choices when you take responsibility for them. Your children need love more than material things, but love doesn't put food in their mouths or a roof over their heads. It is heartbreaking if the decision to provide food, shelter, and clothing is like a multiple-choice question you make daily because you don't have enough money or a place to call home. The other side of that coin is that there is nothing wrong with wanting to live comfortably and give good things to your children. Making sound financial decisions isn't easy if you are starting from ground zero or recovering from a devastating setback, but it is possible. You won't have all the answers, but I can guarantee that you will not have any answers that will improve your financial situation if you don't try.

~SINGLE PARENT 101~
Overcoming Financial Stress

- *Do you need assistance with learning how to create a budget?*

    Consider asking a friend with experience in financial management or someone who seems to do well with their finances. Online resources, such as templates and videos, can give you practical advice and step-by-step plans to get you started. You can also attend free financial planning seminars.

- *What can you do to control your spending and cut unnecessary expenses?*

    Once you have a budget, stick with it! Don't be afraid to have age-appropriate conversations with your children about these changes. Tightening your belt could involve switching grocery stores, saying "no" to some extracurricular activities, or not buying your children the latest and greatest things they want but don't need.

- *Do you need temporary help through financial and housing assistance programs?*

    Check with local agencies to obtain a list of non-profit and governmental assistance programs to see if you qualify. If you are in an emergency, find a local shelter or transitional housing to get immediate help for you and your children.

- *What can you do to increase your income?*

    Lowering your expenses may not solve your problem. If possible, get a part-time job or pursue education grants and assistance for career training. Building a strategy to get out of debt or get ahead will feel manageable with a financial plan in place.

CHAPTER FOUR

Let's Talk It Out

*"There is only one rule for being a good talker –
learn to listen."*
– Christopher Morley

You know that you can talk to me about anything. How popular is this statement on television shows when parents are having a heart-to-heart talk with their children? How popular is it in your home? An even better question is: do you believe that you have cultivated a relationship with your children where they believe that they really can come to you and talk to you about things that matter to them?

When I was pregnant with Cortez, I would talk to him as I watched his little feet push and move across my stomach. I laugh out loud at how terrified I was when I brought him home from the hospital. He was only two weeks early but had to wear preemie diapers for a few weeks because regular diapers slid right off. He was so cute but a fussy little guy who had colic and had his days and nights mixed up for a while. He would cry for hours until close to 2:00 am. He caused me to have sleep deprivation that I can only imagine is achieved when you are held hostage and tortured for top-secret information. I was the walking dead during the first three months of his life. Even with his remarkable vocal performances each night of "Cry Baby" and his brilliant portrayal of "Sleepless in St. Louis," Cortez's dependency on me captivated me. Without being able to speak, he understood my love for him through my words and my interactions. I would coo and talk to him with such confidence that he somehow understood me. I was so in awe of how he talked to me with sounds, gestures, and looks. Over time, I learned the difference between a hungry cry, a diaper change cry, and a cry to get my attention. Hearing my voice or feeling my touch would soothe him, and his little face would tell me when he was happy or sad.

You remember those days. Can you think back to when your children were babies or toddlers and didn't say a word but would put their arms out to you for you to pick them up? You were teaching them how to communicate. You were attentive and listened to their every need, and responded with appropriate words or actions. It is funny that parents understand their toddlers far better than anyone else, and others have to ask for interpretation. What sounds like gibberish is clear and concise to parents, and then parents must translate to others. When raising a teenager, I promise you that Cortez spoke clear and concise English, and I still need someone to translate the latest slang. At sixteen, he told me exactly what he needed and sometimes talked way more than he should, but he still understood my love for him through my words and interactions.

Meaningful Conversations

Cortez has always been a night owl. He is full of energy during a time when most of us are winding down. I'm an early bird, and he liked to sleep late, which was always frustrating. It was a struggle to get him up and moving in the morning for school.

Until he was in 8th grade, he would come into my room some nights to say good night but then spark the most random conversations. I, of course, would be aggravated because I would look around, and it would be past his bedtime by the time the conversation ended. Sometimes I would cut him off and be very rigid about him being in bed at his appointed bedtime. At a point, I decided to pick my battles wisely. Instead of just telling him to go to bed, I told him to try coming down earlier to say good night, even if he wasn't going to lie down at that moment. That didn't work because that next night, he was at my door at 9:30 pm telling me good night. His routine was to climb into bed with me and launch into random conversation. Instead of thinking about why he should be in bed, I gave him my undivided attention. I noticed that his random conversation wasn't very random. He started with a general statement, but shortly after, he would tell me about his day or how he felt about something that happened. I slowly realized that this was how he chose to communicate with me. He would start with something generic, almost like he was trying to get a feel for my mood, and then lead into what he wanted to talk about. When I realized that this was his modus operandi, I began eagerly anticipating and embracing those nights.

I listened and didn't give my opinion unless he asked me directly. If he said something I deemed questionable or felt deserved a deeper conversation, I chose not to dig into it at that moment. Maybe a day later or so, I would lead into a conversation during another time and say something like, "Hey, you remember when you told me about this or that?"

One night during bedtime, he asked me what E-Cigarettes were and then told me about a friend who got caught with some in his backpack. I immediately wanted to drill him and ask, have you ever smoked? Has anyone ever offered you drugs? Did the friend's mother know? Instead of interrogating him, I parked my concern into my mental rolodex and let him finish his story. Two days later, I asked him, "Do you remember when you told me about the E-Cigarettes? Do you have any other questions about them?" Those two questions led to a meaningful and mutually shared interest in discussing harmful drugs and other substances. We have talked about those things in theory throughout his life, but having a real-life scenario that he shared was a very different conversation. My gut feeling was that if I had gone into panic mode that night, he would have shut down and felt he couldn't tell me things like that without getting the third degree or being read the riot act.

That has been my pattern with him for years. Right around eighth grade, he stopped going into those conversations at night. He would kiss me and tell me good night. However, Cortez still talks to me about things that are important to him, including very uncomfortable topics. When we have conflicts, he has come to me and said, "Mom can I talk to you about what happened?"

I'm a problem solver, so I'm always wanting to pick his brain and interrogate him, but when he willingly comes to me to talk about something, I take him seriously, show him that I am listening to him, and trust my instinct on how to deal with it. Yes, I've blown it, but learning from those experiences helped me understand him better.

Actions Don't Always Speak Louder Than Words

Have you heard the saying that "silence is golden"? I found that the old proverb really says, "Speech is silver, silence is golden." There are different understandings of the proverb, but in general, it is meant to convey that speaking is good, but not saying anything is even better. If you put that in the proper context, being quiet helps us choose our words wisely, become better listeners, and allow for self-reflection. Those things are certainly important, but sometimes words not spoken can leave people broken.

My mother was a strict disciplinarian. She was a force to be reckoned with, and my brother and I never disrespected her as kids. While my mother's discipline taught me structure, self-control, and responsibility, it wasn't balanced. We didn't have a nurturing mother-daughter relationship. I did not feel like I could trust her and tell her certain things without fear of punishment or judgment. Talking about things that bother me makes me feel better. Thankfully, I sought to fill that void in a positive way. My grandmother was someone that I could talk to about anything. She would listen and affirm me in ways that made me feel like she was listening and cared about what was in my heart. My mother certainly wasn't anything like Faye Dunaway's portrayal of Joan Crawford in *Mommy Dearest*, but she also wasn't like Phylicia Rashad as the beloved Claire Huxtable from *The Cosby Show*. I did not doubt that my mother loved me, but she didn't always display it in a way that made me feel strongly connected with her. She was about taking care of business, strong-minded, independent, and we didn't make that tender mother-daughter connection until I was an adult. It took time, but we grew very close, developing an intimate bond when she lost her mother and when I was going through my divorce.

    As our love for one another deepened, my mother began to open up and say things that affirmed her love for me. She told me how proud she was of the woman and mother I had become every chance she had, and our times together outshined our prior relationship. We had happy moments when I was growing up, but nothing like the continuous delight we experienced later in life.

    In 2013, my mother died of lung cancer. I miss her deeply. I spent the last year and a half of her life helping care for her while she battled cancer. During the last few months of her life, I worked remotely from the hospital or her home. There was nothing inside of me that felt that it was my duty or obligation. I just loved my mother so much that I didn't know how to respond any other way. I don't know how I would have felt if it happened ten years earlier. Sometimes, she spoke to me as though she didn't deserve my devotion and support. During very intimate conversations, she regretted some of her decisions while raising me as a single mother. While she was thinking about what she could have done better, I was thinking about my life and how much she influenced me and shaped me in areas that people have admired about me.

Every day mattered, but there was one day that sealed my mother's heart and wiped away her regrets. After spending the day at the hospital and planning for her funeral, yes, preparing for her to die, I began packing up my laptop to head home. As I zipped the bag, I began crying uncontrollably after not showing much vulnerability in front of my mother while she was sick. I walked over to her bed, climbed in it, and laid on her chest like a little girl. My mother held me tightly, rubbed my shoulders and arms, kissed me gently on my cheek and forehead, and said, "This is what I've been waiting for. You have been so strong, and I couldn't have asked for a better daughter." She whispered in my ear repeatedly, "I love you." My mother passed away a few months later, and as much as I wanted to rewrite history to have more time with her, losing her inspired me to find my purpose and passion in life. I thought of her often while writing this book and wondered if she would be pleased.

Speaking Their Love Language

Even as an adult, my mother's affirmation meant the world. I wanted a relationship with my father, who wasn't in my life, and I craved my mother's acceptance and affection even though she was a constant in my life.

Children need unconditional love and constant affirmation. Not just any affirmation; they need positive affirmation. I recommend reading the book: *The 5 Love Languages of Children* or *The 5 Love Languages of Teenagers* by Gary Chapman. Children need to hear and feel that you love them. Having an absent parent speaks very loudly to some children. It screams, "You don't love me," "You don't care about me," "You don't want me," or even "You hate me." Feelings of rejection and abandonment can cut deep, but feelings of being neglected or unloved in the home can cut even deeper. Learning how your children like to express and receive love can open the lines of communication and help you connect with them on a deeper level. For example, Cortez's primary love language is affirmation. He feels most loved by hearing uplifting words. Conversely, he is wounded by condemning words. Abrasive words can hurt anyone to a certain degree, but if affirmation is your love language, those words cut a little deeper. Telling him that I'm disappointed with him because of a choice he made mostly gets his attention easier than giving him my "I am the parent, hear me roar" voice. My primary love language is acts of service, so when Cortez does his chores, I'm on cloud nine. On the other hand, I've learned that I can overreact when he fails to do a tiny chore. It would be nice if our children knew our love language. For example, when Cortez sends a text asking permission to do something, the last part of the message usually ends with "I've done my chores." Doing chores is a house rule, so he doesn't have to tell me that, but I think he knew subconsciously that I would be in a better mood when I got home.

Effective communication begins with listening. As parents, you sometimes dismiss your children's opinions, thoughts, and emotions. Paying attention to their body language and other non-verbal expressions is a skill that isn't automatically implanted. At the core of most misunderstandings and disagreements is a communication breakdown. Men and women communicate differently and having two parents can provide a balanced approach to building good communication skills in a family. As single parents, you can teach your children how to communicate effectively, and you can teach them by modeling effective communication in your homes.

How hard has it been for you? You may have excellent communication with your children. If so, keep up the good work. There may be certain situations or seasons when communication has been challenging. You are making a difference even if your children's responses to your efforts don't make you feel like you are. If good communication is not happening, now is the time to try to engage your children. I know that you carry the entire load of managing your home. Sometimes you get tired, frustrated, stressed, overwhelmed, and may even have a misguided focus when prioritizing family needs. I can't promise it will be easy, but it will be worth it when you create an atmosphere of honest, open, and safe communication in your home.

I began this chapter with the famous statement, "You know that you can talk to me about anything." Remember that nobody talks to anyone about everything. When priorities change, and situations may demand more of your attention, what do you sacrifice: quality or quantity? Both are important, but if your quantity of time with your children is spent with you on social media while they are texting, there is no honest, meaningful communication occurring. I'm not saying you should abandon technology, but I am saying that quality time with your children is priceless. It creates a strong connection. Quality time invites opportunities to engage with them, talk about the day, and affirm that you care and are listening.

The absence of a parent or even the inconsistent time spent by the other parent can have an emotional impact on children. Divorce, death, and other life changes can be tough. Your best attempts are to build loving, trusting, and respectful relationships with your children so they feel safe and comfortable talking with you about things that matter to them.

Good communication is the only way to understand your children's view of their single-parent home. The impact on each child might be different, but there is a good chance that your child can have a deeper connection with you when they know their feelings about their family are important. The communication and attention of one parent who is tenacious about raising their children with family values can leave a legacy for the next generation of their family.

~SINGLE PARENT 101~
Improving Communication

- *What can you do to improve the communication between you and your children?*

    Try communicating through family time activities. Let your children pick activities that they enjoy. Surprisingly, I sat with my son and let him show me how to play one of his sports video games. Our conversations are light-hearted and fun.

- *What do you do if your child is distant or unresponsive to your attempts to communicate?*

    No matter how hard you try, sometimes your children will not open up to you. Having them speak to a counselor at school or a professional counselor might help with reaching them when they start to display outwardly that something serious is troubling them, and you can't seem to connect with them to get to the heart of the matter.

- *How can you encourage your children to express themselves?*

    Introduce alternative ways to share their feelings, such as journaling. If they have a particular interest, learn more about it and ask open-ended questions to spark meaningful conversations.

- *How can I keep the lines of communication open as they get older?*

    The best thing any parent can do is listen to your children without judgment and then use wisdom in responding. From the youngest to the oldest, children are still people, and they want to feel like they are being heard. Boundaries need to be enforced so that they understand what is unacceptable or disrespectful.

CHAPTER FIVE

Flying Solo

"The only time we waste is the time we spend thinking we are alone."
– Mitch Albom

A man was shocked to see his beautiful neighbor knocking on his door one Friday evening. "I'm feeling so lonely that I can't stand it," she said. "I want to go out and get drunk and want to enjoy my life. Are you free tonight?"

"Yes," he replied enthusiastically.

"Wonderful," she said. "Would you watch my kids?"

I literally laughed out loud when I first read this piece. In full disclosure, besides wanting to get drunk, I have wanted to get out or get away from my kid. What has it been like for you? You are all too familiar with being overwhelmed and lonely, and those adjectives might even be an understatement. I touched on loneliness earlier, but let's go deeper. You can probably sense loneliness creeping up on you like a thief in the night to steal your joy and fulfillment of being around your children. Usually, when you use the phrase 24/7 to describe time, it is an exaggeration, but who wants most of the time away from their children occurring when they are sleeping or at school?

It's not that I didn't do things to enjoy life; it's just that more of my time was spent doing a lot for my son in his early years. If you are in a relationship with a significant other living with you, this may not apply to you. Even if you are in a relationship and don't live with the other person, you can hit the walls of loneliness. Being lonely doesn't always come from not having someone in your presence. Feelings of loneliness can come from the frustration of being alone in raising your children. I've been married, and I've had family live with me. If your marriage or relationship isn't good, there is still something to be said about having an abled-bodied person around to do this while you do that. Your children can be in your face all day long, but your loneliness can stem from missing the help of another parent.

Loneliness is just one of many battles that you contend with while being a single parent. It is impossible to create a comprehensive list of struggles you encounter while raising children, but social isolation and loneliness are at the top. "You are not alone" may sound like a generic cliché but trust me when I tell you it is not, and I am communicating that from a sincere and compassionate heart. I know that feelings of being alone and lonely in parenting can be a different emotion than the loneliness felt from not being married or dating. Both types of loneliness can be overwhelming.

I Didn't Plan for This

The first time I spoke with Tony Fonte about his eleven-year-old daughter Kailee, I could hear his devotion to her. He was passionate in sharing how he moved forward after losing his wife. Kailee was only five years old when her mother died. Tony isn't shy about revealing that the man and father he is today came out of a place of deep brokenness. Unlike divorce, which is a choice, becoming a single parent for Tony wasn't a decision he made willingly. Not only was he dealing with grief; he became a single dad and had to try to adjust to the challenges of raising a daughter. His mother died two years after his wife, and his father and brother had major health challenges. Tony was miserable, not just because he had suffered so much loss and pain, but because he had other things that went on in his childhood that he brought into adulthood that he didn't like about himself. He wanted to be a great dad to Kailee, but he was angry and bitter. He was overwhelmed with trauma, trying to be a single parent, and struggling to make each day meaningful.

Tony spoke about failing miserably many times until his life was transformed by a piercing moment of self-awareness that he needed to change. He knew his daughter was watching him, so he went on a mission to become the best dad he could be. He didn't just decide to change; he changed by being vulnerable and open about his struggles to the men holding him accountable and helping him through that difficult time. His turning point was when his mentor, a pastor, talked to him about being healed of his past hurts, disappointments, and failures. Tony worked on being healed and identified the kind of man and father he wanted to be. That is where he put his focus. Over time, the man he saw staring back in the mirror was a man his daughter could be proud to call her dad.

Tony is now an author and speaker who teaches men to embrace vulnerability and use that to become the best dads, husbands, and leaders they can possibly be. He explained, "Men are wired to think that vulnerability is a weakness and not to ask for help. We are taught to believe that we must be providers, do everything independently, and have all the answers. This is so far from the truth. Men should be providers, but not at the expense of being cold and callous to life circumstances."

Acknowledging and asking for help wasn't a sign of weakness for him. It was one of his strongest decisions for himself and his daughter. Tony relied on his faith in God, his circle of mentors, and Kailee's grandmother. He surrounded himself with like-minded people who encouraged and supported him. He isn't aiming for perfection and admits that one of his challenges is still being able to show Kailee the more delicate and nurturing emotions while providing the wisdom that daughters receive from their mothers. He balances that by learning from her. They understand the importance and significance of being honest with each other. He apologizes when he doesn't quite meet her need in the nurturing area, and she tells him when she needs more than what he gives. Kailee's grandmother helps care for her when Tony is working. She sees her daughter in her granddaughter and loves to show her a tenderness that would have come from her mother. Tony candidly shares their story in his book: *New Beginnings: Step into the Life You Were Created to Live.* Having support as a single parent is so important, and Tony encouraged me by saying, "We can learn so much from our kids. It's been a scary roller coaster and a fun ride at the same time because I've learned so much as a parent."[1]

I know that single moms are the majority, but it is a tragedy that, generally, as a society, we are dismissive of the importance of dads in the home. Like many other single parents, Tony learned to embrace his role as a single dad.

Me, Myself, and I

"She has no clue what it's like to do this alone." A frustrated single mother commented this about another mother who thought the world was ending because her husband was on a business trip, and she had to handle everything alone. With one eyebrow raised and my head somewhat shaking in agreement, I knew her comment made complete sense. Interestingly, the next sentence out of my mouth completely contradicted my outward gestures.

"I don't know, I think the fact that she is overwhelmed seems about right," was my response.

You have been around parents who have voiced their frustrations about carrying out tasks for the entire household and feeling like the world's weight was on their shoulders while their spouses were gone. You may have found yourself giving the blank stare and thinking "Welcome to my single-parent life of doing it alone".

As much as doing it alone seems to be an exact definition of single parenting, not every situation is truly a solo endeavor. There are different kinds of situations, and I have been on both ends of the spectrum. I was not married to Cortez's dad when I got pregnant. We were living together, eventually married, and later divorced. I was a full-time single mother for most of his life. Certain internal struggles are more prevalent when one parent is solely responsible for raising children. I've touched on the financial strain, but loneliness is also at the top.

The word "single" shrieks of someone being by themselves or alone. Me, myself, and I might sound strong and convincing when it comes to single dating, but it doesn't work so well for parenting. For this reason, the saying that it takes a village to raise a child should always be in full swing for us.

My mother was a part of my village and losing her created an indescribable void in many areas of my life. My grandmother was vital to my mother's village while raising me. However, the village does not always have to be relatives. My circle of support was not that large, but it consisted of my male relatives, women who are like sisters and a select few of those women's husbands who were willing to invest in my son's life and provide support for him when I needed a man's influence.

Who is in your village? Your decision to allow others into your circle of trust in child rearing helps your children and gives you the support and encouragement you need. Let your village know how much you appreciate them. You are blessed if you have special people, family, or friends committed to standing alongside you.

Tag Team

For many years, Cortez has been a wrestling fan. One of the wrestling events is usually a tag team. A tag team is a pair of wrestlers who fight their opponents, taking the ring alternately. One team member can only enter the ring once touched or tagged by the one leaving. Feeling lonely as a single parent is a lot like tag team wrestling, except you don't have a person to tag. When the other parent isn't your tag team partner, looking to your village is the next best thing. It may feel uncomfortable and embarrassing asking for help, but it can bless your socks off when you do.

When Cortez was in the 4th grade, I checked his backpack after school and found a crumpled-up colorful flyer. When I unfolded the paper, it read, "Donuts with Dad." This was an event at his school similar to "Muffins with Mom," where the appropriate parent gets singled out to have breakfast with their children before school. It was heartbreaking to see that he had balled it up and didn't even show it to me. When I asked him about it, he said, "Why does it matter? There is no one here to take me."

He even went as far as to say, "Why don't I have a second dad like other families."

We spent a moment talking about the situation. He just shrugged it off like it was no big deal, but I couldn't help but wonder how he felt about the situation. Parents must know their children's heart on certain matters and sometimes try to read their non-verbal language. As the evening went on, the situation troubled me. I began to think about the men in our lives and who might be willing to take him. I almost talked myself out of even considering the idea because I wanted a man who would leave an impression on him and not make him feel weird around other kids with their dads.

The perfect man came to mind. I dialed his number, and sure enough, he was happy to hear from me. The voice on the other end of the phone was Cortez's great-grandfather. My granddad was elated that I had called him and asked him to take Cortez to Donuts with Dad. My granddad came the next night, had dinner with us, and took Cortez to school for the occasion. Cortez was excited to introduce his great-grandfather to his friends, and my grandfather was proud to stand in the gap. This was such a special time for them.

Donuts with Dad was one of my decisions to fight for my son. I was fighting against feeling like I had to do things alone and fighting for my son to know that although his father had let him down, good men around him loved and cared for him. Boys need to have positive male role models in the absence of a father.

You Are Not Alone

Times of loneliness are legitimate when nobody is there to help carry the load. I often found myself simply wishing that someone else were there to do this so that I could do that. What always keeps me going is the fact that I was not alone. My son was also going through this journey with me. As much as I felt alone, I had to remember that he was also along for the ride. He was hitting speed bumps of his own that he may not have been able to communicate.

You are in the ring of life daily and responsible for making all the decisions for your children. I know there are days when you have felt like you have been body-slammed, kicked, punched, and smacked in the face. It would be great if you had a hand to tag to leave the ring. If you don't have a partner to tag, there is nothing wrong with getting out of the ring, but you do have to get back in so you don't get counted out. I've learned to take care of myself and find times to be refreshed. I get massages, talk long walks, and spend time with my sista-friends with whom I can laugh and cry. These are just a few things that I like to do to recharge. I plan my life around doing these things instead of waiting until I am completely depleted and worn out. Take time to find those activities, people, or quiet moments that can restore you to get back in the ring.

Nothing can justify walking away from parental responsibility. Even if someone else abandoned them or if they lost a dad or mom, help your children thrive by creating a circle of support.

A woman can never be a father, and a man can never be a mother to a child. You cannot completely fill the hole left when one parent is absent. The gift you can give your children in the absence of another parent is your best version of yourself and surround them with people you trust who are willing to support you and invest in their future. Your village may exist with little effort from you because you have people who are there for you organically. For others, it may take some effort to develop. You win the battle by making the best of every situation. Even if you are the only person in your child's corner right now, you have what it takes to see them through their childhood journey into adulthood.

~SINGLE PARENT 101~
Dealing With Loneliness

- *Who is in your village?*

    In most cases, relatives are often the primary source of support for single parents. Don't be afraid or too prideful to ask for help, especially from trusted family members and friends who have communicated that they are there for you. You can additionally connect with other parents through athletic and social activities or join a single-parent advocacy group for support.

- *How can you balance managing your home?*

    If finances are not an issue, the sky's the limit. You can hire babysitters, housekeepers, and the like to help you. Since this is not the case for most single parents, enlist family or your older children to help babysit, but make sure it's not too burdensome. Children should have household chores. It's two-fold because it helps you and it teaches them responsibility.

- *What can you do to overcome feelings of loneliness?*

    When I feel lonely, I shift my thinking to positive thoughts, or I do something productive to get my mind off what I know is a temporary moment in my day or time in my life. If you have little kids, take trips to the park where they can play, or you can have your baby in a stroller while you enjoy a change in scenery. You can also take the edge off by spending time with family and friends.

- *How do you handle loneliness when your children are away?*

    This is the time to learn how to manage your emotions and understand how to care for yourself. Use alone time to recharge and rest. Find activities that you enjoy and commit to them. When your children are away, it's a great time to get caught up on things to do around the house or plan for the upcoming week to ease the stress.

CHAPTER SIX

Count the Cost

"While we are free to choose our actions, we are not free to choose the consequences of our actions."
– Stephen R. Covey

You won't hear many people say, "I'm the way I am because I grew up without a father." You probably won't catch too many individuals declaring, "I treat you the way I do because my mother was never around." It's not uncommon for adults to struggle in relationships or outwardly display some dysfunction because they were raised by a single parent or in a home where one or both of their parents failed them. My rejection from my father deserting me led me to stay in an emotionally damaging relationship. I didn't want to be subjected to the pain of someone discarding me like yesterday's trash, as my father did. It took several years for me to heal from those devastating wounds.

When a parent chooses to be absent from their child's life, they have no idea how far-reaching the consequence extends when making that choice. In many cases, walking away from their children has no immediate consequence, and leaving the other parent shouldering the responsibility doesn't affect them at all. An involuntary message is that the action or decision to abandon a child has no real consequences. It would be best to teach your children early to recognize that their good or bad decisions have consequences.

Sticky Situations

When Cortez was in elementary school, we used to read a book called *Sticky Situations* by Betsy Schmitt.[1] It is a Christian devotional; each day, it gives an age-appropriate situation and provides multiple-choice answers to discuss together. The book provides a bible verse at the end of each discussion to help direct the conversation and teach your child how to apply biblical principles to ordinary life circumstances. Although there was always one answer that fundamentally followed the Bible, to Cortez, not all of the other answers were blatantly wrong. There were times when Cortez didn't initially make the best choice, but after discussing the consequences of each choice, he eventually understood that there was a "right" answer.

Cortez was learning that he will face moral or ethical situations that demand a "right" choice, and "right" is based on absolute truth. If he must choose between the truth and a lie, the choice is black and white; tell the truth because the circumstances surrounding the issue aren't relevant. He was also learning that there will be situations that won't challenge him morally, but those situations also demand a "right" choice. The "right" choice isn't always black and white. Between black and white are shades of gray, which make teaching children about choices and consequences important for all parents.

I've struggled with the gray choices and making decisions for my son without his father. Being in that position leaves very little room to be indecisive and unsure. Being the only parent teaching my son about choices and consequences was sometimes daunting, but I tried to use it to establish trust, communication, and respect.

Standing by Our Decisions

Cortez's friends always enjoyed hanging out at our house. It wasn't often, but when the tables were turned, I went into FBI mode when he would ask to spend the night at a friend's house whom I didn't know very well. When he was twelve, there was one situation where I felt comfortable allowing him to attend a sleepover because I spoke to the mother over the phone and met the father when I dropped him off. A few boys were sleeping over for a birthday, which made me feel good about my decision. A few days later, while checking Cortez's phone, I found a video he shot at the sleepover. As the camera spanned around this gathering that included a lot more adults than I was made aware of, I saw adults drinking alcohol and heard inappropriate language being used. I will be the first to tell you that what you choose to do in your own house is your business, but when you care for someone else's children, you need to use wiser judgment. Some of these adults were clearly intoxicated.

When I sat with Cortez, watched the video, and began talking with him, he was very defensive and didn't seem to understand why it bothered me. My overly passionate response was, "Cortez, I would have never allowed you to go over there if I knew those things were happening." I could have stopped there, but I let my emotions get the best of me and went into a rant, asking, "What else went on that wasn't in the video" and saying, "I can't believe his parents would permit this type of mess to go on with other teenagers in their care." I knew I had lost him when I was done having my little tantrum.

His dry and dispassionate response was, "Not everyone's family is like ours."

Let's just say that conversation ended with me saying, "Don't worry, you are not going over there again."

I was upset that he was indifferent about the situation. I was frustrated that he seemingly felt comfortable hearing that type of language. I was angry that I allowed him to go even though I did my due diligence beforehand. I felt he would have been okay with being in that environment again if I had given him the green light.

A few weeks passed before we had a chance to discuss it again. He asked if he could go back to this young man's house, and my answer was, "No," followed, by his question, "Why not? My friend said his dad doesn't always drink like that when his friends are over." To make a long story short, I explained to him that I wasn't attacking his friend's family or trying to say that we were better than they were. I painted a picture of some things that could have gone wrong if this young man's parents were drinking and chose to drive with all of them in the car. I played out some other worst-case scenarios with him and highlighted the consequences of drinking irresponsibly. When you tell your children to do something that you don't put into practice and sometimes blatantly throw in their faces when you act irresponsibly, they lose respect for you, and your authority in your home is weakened. It just so happens that I choose not to drink alcohol around children, but if I did and were reckless, my message to Cortez would have little to no impact.

The light bulb didn't go on right away, and I could tell that he still struggled with my decision because of peer pressure or feeling like he was the only one that wasn't going. Keep in mind that I didn't forbid him from being friends with the young man. I simply did not allow him to engage with this friend in an environment that I deemed unsafe. Needless to say, he survived that day, and I haven't heard that young man's name again.

Even if I ran my choices for Cortez by a relative or good friend, I was ultimately accountable for the outcome. Going into a shell, letting Cortez continue to hang out, and hoping he would be unaffected by drunkenness and foul language wasn't an option for me. I can't shield him from everything, but I'm not going to place him in harmful circumstances willingly. Does Cortez see and hear inappropriate things? Of course, he does, but it won't be with my consent because I didn't feel like making the tough decision that day.

I like sharing this example because it also gives me a glimpse of my responsibility to make good choices. I didn't check my son's phone daily, but I checked it often enough. The message isn't to start spying on your children every chance you get. The message is that when you face a difficult situation with your children, you don't get to pass the buck to the other parent or agree on how to deal with things. I could have ignored or dismissed what happened at the sleepover and hoped it never happened again. Consequences work both ways. Your children have consequences for their choices, and you have consequences for how you handle them. I've tried to be consistent with reward and punishment with my son, and sometimes I've won the battle and lost the war. Picking your battles wisely is easier said than done, especially when you are the only one choosing those battles. You can get advice from all over the place, and you will hear everything from "Let your children fail, take away what matters to them the most" or even the popular "it's my way or the highway" approach. The truth is that you can't keep grasping for straws and shadowboxing with your children when it comes to consequences. They will face them in and outside of your home, so they must learn about the significance of their decisions.

Look for the Positives

While having two parents in the home to confront choices and consequences is ideal, be encouraged because the advantage you have is that you don't have to contend with another parent's opposing position on child-rearing. Division can exist in marriages and relationships when parents don't agree on these issues. You can be courageous and strong in teaching your children the importance of making good decisions.

Bouncing ideas off one another and working together to make decisions for children is one of the advantages of being in a two-parent home. Everyday interaction in a two-parent household, whether intentional or not, can give children conflicting outlooks on being good decision-makers. You could model consistent and responsible choices. Being consistent and responsible doesn't mean that you're always right. Sometimes consistent and responsible might involve taking responsibility for and dealing with the consequences of bad choices. Learning to make good decisions can be draining, but as children mature and make their own choices, they can have integrity and understand the cost of the consequences.

Don't beat yourself up when you make bad choices. The guilt is not as severe when you and the other parent decide together, and it goes sideways, but the guilt is increased when you make the decision alone and it doesn't turn out well. Apologizing to your children and admitting that you dropped the ball is a compelling way for your children to see first-hand that you are not perfect and make bad decisions too.

Don't freak out when your kids make bad choices. Although you can't always depend on another person to enforce consequences, you can teach and encourage your children to make good choices. When they make that choice the first time, you can swoop in and teach them what is and is not acceptable behavior and what will happen to them if they make that choice again. Get into the habit of creating teachable moments, so you don't overreact to every wrong decision. You can learn to evaluate the severity of a wrong choice so that you are not making light of a serious concern that must be addressed.

It can be challenging for any parent to teach consequences when children are older. Even well-prepared parents can have strong-willed children that rebel just for the sake of doing so. I once heard someone say, "Conduct permitted is conduct taught."[2] Your goal is to raise good decision-makers, and sometimes the guilt you carry for being the only parent causes you to overcompensate in other areas, such as not making your children accountable for their decisions. You don't want to fall into that trap. I felt like the responsibility of making decisions is never ending and carrying the burden of those outcomes is sometimes heavy. I had to get creative in teaching my son about his choices and consequences.

The Rules of the Game

Cortez is an intelligent, handsome, funny, and outgoing young man. Let me stress how funny and outgoing he is for a moment. Throughout his education, Cortez had more female teachers than males. Each time he began the school year with a bang, teachers constantly melted over his smile, outgoing personality, and charm. Although he was intelligent, by the end of the school year, I would get comments that Cortez laughed too much in class. When he was younger, he would receive less-than-desirable behavior marks for his comical and distracting activities in the classroom.

Frustrated that my verbal and non-verbal communication weren't getting through to him, I considered another approach. I eventually recognized that the issue was that when teachers were lenient with him, he would push the envelope and take advantage. It came down to the fact that he was not respecting the teacher's authority.

My next conversation with him was different. Cortez was a football player. He has played either flag or tackle football since third grade and has a good knowledge of the game. Regarding his behavior, I painted a picture of authority to him using a football analogy.

- **Every team has an owner** — *We are a team, and God owns our team. Through the Bible and His relationship with the head coach, God establishes the mission and provides the focus, guidance, and standards of excellence necessary to succeed in the League of Life.*
- **Every team has a head coach** — *I am the head coach of our team, and I am responsible for managing the team. I outline the goals, create the system, and give direction to*

the team. I communicate the expectations and disciplines for how the team will operate.

- **Every team has assistant coaches** — *Teachers, instructors, and others in authority are my assistant coaches. They support me in managing my team and can execute in my absence.*
- **Every team has a captain** — *Cortez is the team's captain and is responsible for executing the plays and being a leader for the other players on the team. One day he is the quarterback, another day, he might be the running back, but he is expected to play whatever position is needed to win the game.*
- **Every team has a playbook** — *The playbook contains the description and diagrams of the plays and strategies the coach and assistant coaches created. Our team's playbook has hundreds of plays that have been communicated and executed since Cortez was little, but Cortez also could call an audible if a situation requires him to use better judgment. An audible is a tactic in football where the play can be changed to adjust to the defense.*
- **Every game has rules** — *Good behavior is a first down, a touchdown, or a field goal. Bad behavior is either a fumble, interception or a penalty. Obeying the rules will result in positive yards or a score and*

disobeying them will result in negative yards or a score by the other team.

Using this analogy and putting teachers in the same light as his assistant coaches made a light bulb go on for Cortez. I knew first-hand how Cortez controlled himself with his football coaches because he respected their authority. I can't tell you how many times and in how many ways I tried to communicate that his teachers deserve the same respect that he showed me, but in this case, it was literally like I was saying it for the first time, and he was hearing it for the first time.

His behavior didn't change overnight, but I communicated with him so that he could receive the message. Over the next year or so, with consistent delivery of the message and consequences, I saw a fantastic effort and, eventually, significant changes in his classroom behavior. His teachers boasted about him making good choices and removing himself from situations with friends that could disrupt the classroom. Don't get me wrong, he was not perfect by any means, and none of us are, but he matured by leaps and bounds.

I gave this example because I assumed I effectively communicated with Cortez. He was certainly hearing me, but he wasn't listening, and quite honestly, I wasn't listening to him either. I was doing a lot of reacting but not listening.

My method for resolving the issue wasn't altogether random. I'm meticulous, and there is usually a method to my madness. I know how my kid is wired. He was not that kid that needed to be spanked all the time. I knew chastising him to death wouldn't change him in this situation, although he has had his share of spankings and punishments. After listening to his explanations for why he continued his conduct and considering that my consequences weren't working, I had to reflect on his personality and how I could reach him. Through intentional listening, I could hear that he did not respect passive and less authoritative teachers to the degree that he respected other adults.

My example was detailed; you don't have to be Inspector Gadget like me. James Dobson, the founder of "Focus on the Family," once stated how, "The child should know what is and is not acceptable behavior before he is held responsible for those rules." That's the formula, and sometimes you must start back at square one with your children. You don't have the luxury of having someone else in the home to share the responsibility of communicating the rules or the consequences when there is a breakdown in communication with your children. Still, you can trust that when you are consistent, children learn.

~SINGLE PARENT 101~
Making Decisions

- *What are some of the benefits of teaching your children about making decisions?*

    If you don't teach your children about making decisions, society will choose for them. Understanding how to make decisions helps children be more responsible, confident, and good leaders.

- *How do you teach your children to become good decision-makers?*

    Finding the right approach to teaching your children to make good decisions is complicated. While there may be more than one method, they all share two major things. Teaching your children about decisions will require that they understand choices and consequences. Another important factor is for you to follow through with the choices that you've given them.

- *When not in a crisis, do you talk with your children about good and bad choices?*

    You don't have to wait to teach the lessons. Hypothetical scenarios, especially at a young age, are a great way to help your children learn to make good decisions. This can be done through board games, talking with them about something on television, or asking them how they would respond to a situation they witnessed.

- *When do you allow your children to fail?*

    Watching your children fail can be grueling. You must make the tough decisions and be at peace with your choice. Children learn from their mistakes just like you do. Serious consequences that would cause harm or that can't be reversed can be a good gauge for intervening. It's more complicated than that, but your intuition will kick in if you start there.

CHAPTER SEVEN

Do as I Say, Not as I Do

"Children are great imitators. So give them something great to imitate."

– Anonymous

One of the elements of having a two-parent household, and it's not always an advantage, is that you can have two people collaborating on different parenting styles and two people modeling behavior. The benefits to children who observe a caring father and a mother interacting in the home daily are widely documented. With so many other societal influences, I consider it advantageous to have two parents in the home who are not just speaking their values and expectations but also modeling good parenting for their children. From birth, children intuitively imitate one or both parents. Good or bad, you are their unofficial role models.

What is good parenting anyway? Is it so subjective that there is no standard? Let's look at one definition of good parenting that gives a practical reference point.

Good parenting happens when a person creates a stable, nurturing home environment for a child, is a positive role model, and plays a positive and active part in a child's life.[1] Good parents provide moral and spiritual guidance, set limits, and provide consequences for a child's behavior. Good parents accept responsibility for the child's total development and guide the child in making sound, healthy life decisions through open communication and mutual respect.[2]

Contrary to the popular beliefs of today's culture regarding gender, men and women are different. As parents, a father and mother bring distinctive characteristics, unique capabilities, and special significance to a child's life, yet they also bring unity and oneness to their parental roles. You are on the hook to do the work it takes to be a good parent if the other parent isn't around or is not committed to co-parenting with you. What your children see in your behavior matters a great deal. If you are not deliberate with your behavior, you can send involuntary messages to your children. For example, the domino theory is a cumulative effect produced when one event sets off a chain of similar events. I don't want my son to abandon his children or divorce. If he chooses to marry, I want him to be a wonderful husband and a loving father to his children. I don't want to produce generations of single parents and have that become normal or the goal. I don't want to leave that legacy. Could my son end up being a single father? Sure, he could, and it wouldn't be the worst thing in the world, but that is not the plan. Would anyone intentionally plan or design their life so that their children would have the same struggles they did if it were unpleasant or painful? By nature, most people acquiesce to the idea of giving their children a better life than they had. Nevertheless, I'm living out the domino effect and taking a stand to break my family's cycle of single-parent homes.

Perhaps you come from a very loving and stable home with married parents. Perhaps you come from a hostile and unstable home with married parents. Maybe you didn't have either parent, grew up in foster homes, or were adopted. What would it look like if you could choose a life for your children? Wouldn't you like to see your daughter or son meet the right person, marry, and have children? I know it would be a personal choice, but let's dream for a moment. Your children may not aspire to marry or have children, which is okay. If they do, you want to do your best to be a role model and gift them with words that they can hear and actions they can see that represent the values that you are trying to teach them. That approach will benefit them as individuals even if marriage and children are not part of their life's journey.

Playing the Hand

You have seen movies or people you know whose children prefer one parent to the other because mom or dad is more lenient. I was a huge *Leave It to Beaver* fan, a show from the late 1950s and 1960s. Before you think too hard, I wasn't born yet, but I watched syndicated shows when I was young. Even as a child, I appreciated how June Cleaver, the wife, could tell her children consistently that their father would deal with them when he got home.

When I was growing up, and I'm sure my brother would agree, I would have much rather had a choice than to only deal with my mother. In my home, Cortez does not have a choice either. He has to play the hand that he was dealt. I am the only authority in our home, and the only person Cortez can look to for consent. He can pick up on the type of mood I'm in without me saying too much because, like most people, I have a tell like in poker. I'm not a poker player, but I love the idea of a tell. A tell in poker is a change in a player's behavior or demeanor claimed by some to give clues to that player's assessment of their hand. A player gains an advantage if they observe and understand the meaning of another player's tell, particularly if the tell is unconscious and reliable. I have a tell that can give Cortez an idea about my mood so he can gain an advantage on his approach with me. My life is one big tell. My choices, behavior, and lifestyle give others clues about my true character and the values that are important to me.

Consider the opening quote of this chapter about your children imitating you. As a parent, your life is one big tell to your children; they are watching you. Studies show that the human brain increases to 80% of its adult size between birth and three years.[3] At that age, kids are like sponges; they soak up information from their surroundings. Little children are not the only ones like sponges; pre-teens and teenagers soak up your actions, dispositions, and attitudes. They are watching your conduct and responses, and by default, you give them reliable evidence of who you are as a human being. My choices, behavior, and lifestyle are like a second parent to Cortez. Those aspects of my life are important because I consider my actions as a second reaffirming voice to him.

Your values and integrity are essential aspects of your life regardless of your marital status or if you have children. I'm not minimizing your responsibility. I am saying that your children are getting one perspective on expected behavior from you, so make it count.

I don't have any numbers to support my theory, but I doubt that the "do as I say, not as I do" parenting style has had much success. The situations can be wide-ranging, from something as seemingly insignificant as telling your children to eat vegetables when you are not eating them to something as significant as telling them not to smoke while lighting a cigarette. You don't want to live contradictory lives by telling them not to curse while you consistently use foul language or something more explosive, like teaching your children to respect others, but you have volatile relationships and display many levels of disrespect.

I try to show up for my son with integrity, not perfection. He has seen my tears of joy and pain. I accept responsibility for changes, challenges, and mistakes. I live my life with faith in Jesus Christ, and I try to create healthy traditions that instill family values that he will take with him when he leaves my home.

I'm hopeful that these statements mean something to you. If you can identify with them, I'm celebrating you and applauding you to stay strong and continue being passionate and intentional about your journey. If you can't relate to those statements, I encourage you to change your thoughts today. One of my favorite quotes is, "When you change your thoughts, you change your world." If you can conceive thoughts of seeing yourself in improved situations, you can change and become the parent you desire to be.

Choices, Behavior, and Lifestyle

A social learning theory claims that people learn through observing, imitating, and modeling. It shows that people not only learn by being rewarded or punished, but they can also learn from watching somebody else being rewarded or punished. These experiments led to more profound studies on the effects of too much television and violent video games. If video games and movies are believed to impact behavior, I am persuaded that what we see or don't see in the home is just as powerful.

I've done or said something I regret in front of my son. Maybe you have too. You may even have a pattern of behavior that you know they are emulating, and at the very least, it doesn't represent the proper standards you want to teach them. Forgiving yourself is a great gift you can give to yourself and your children. There are no do-overs, and you can't change the past, but you can create a fresh start by living a lifestyle that your children can learn from and respect.

You care about your children's attitude and their opinions about you. Not every situation warrants an explanation, but every explanation stems from a desire to teach or correct behavior. With younger children, it is a little different. However, balancing helping them develop positive behavioral responses and dealing with misbehavior can still be hard and challenging, especially when they model your conduct. Your children should be watching your behavior more than they are watching someone else's. There is never a way to know how your children will process the behavior that they see. You can be a great parent, and your children will grow up and make choices that don't reflect the principles you taught them. This truth is not an excuse to live recklessly in front of your children. Instead, it is to bring awareness that you set the foundation.

In the book, *The 7 Habits of Highly Successful People*, author Stephen Covey said, "We see the world, not as it is, but as we are — or, as we are conditioned to see it."[4] Do you see yourself as a good role model for your children? Please take one minute to reflect on that question because you provide a standard they may emulate.

You already know the unflattering statistics of children raised in single-parent homes. Along with those statistics comes a stigma or a perception that single parents, moms in particular, are bad for society or are problems that must be fixed. For years, humiliation by people who disapproved came as generalizations and stereotypes. Single mothers are promiscuous, uneducated, welfare recipients, broke, or intentionally trapped men. Today, whether you are a single mom or a single dad, stereotypes ring to the tune that you cannot be successful parents and successful in other endeavors. A more interesting bias is that society condemns single moms while adoring single dads.

You can't avoid being labeled by others, but how you view yourself plays a vital role in how you show up for your children. It impacts what your children believe about themselves and their circumstances. I want you to see the world as it is, not based on your past choices, behaviors, or experiences.

You are a single parent. How you got here becomes less important when you accept that you are here now. It would be best not to live in guilt or condemnation for your choices. Whether you have one or six children with four different fathers, children are a blessing, and not one child conceived is ever a mistake.

Whatever happened before you picked up this book, when you put it down, I want you to believe you can be a strong parent. Make no mistake, how you see yourself will manifest in ways that will be visible to your children. Remember, you aren't trying to wear capes or leap buildings in single bounds. You are living daily to build a family framework to help your children move beyond what society says they can do. You are not the sum of one, two, three, or however many bad decisions you've made. Let your children see you being a loving parent with a healthy outlook. Your behavior and what you say provide a double dose of effective parenting and can strengthen your core family values.

~SINGLE PARENT 101~
Modeling Behavior

- *Have you identified your parenting style?*

    Your parenting style plays an important role in modeling behavior with your children. You don't have a tag team partner to force or reinforce your parental guidelines. Determine if you are too passive or authoritative in what you say and do. Be willing to make changes.

- *Are there things you do or don't do that contribute to behavioral issues?*

    Remember that your little ones are sponges, and they soak up everything. Your pre-teens and teens are old enough to judge character, and they have front-row seats to your daily life. Your consistent actions that match what you say can strengthen expectations and values with your children when the other parent is not contributing.

- *How often do you evaluate other forces that are driving behavior?*

    Everything from television shows to video games and friends contributes to your children's behavior. Other life changes can be unsettling, such as divorce or remarriage, losing a loved one, and having a new addition to the family. Don't panic but be attentive when there are sudden changes in behavior.

- *How can you show up with integrity – not perfection?*

    Making mistakes in anything is inevitable. I can give examples of where I made mistakes in every significant phase of parenting. I now consider most of them very small in the big scheme. I believe my son will remember how I lived with integrity more than he will anything else. My integrity says, "I'm sorry, son, I should not have handled the situation that way." My integrity is also seen when I stick to my decision and enforce a consequence.

CHAPTER EIGHT

It's Not About Me

"But the greatest of these is love."
– 1 Corinthians 13:13b (NIV)

It is incredible to experience life as a human being, but it is grandiose to carry a human life inside you and deliver that life into this world. Surprisingly, giving birth to a child is not the greatest of deeds that is praiseworthy. Raising a child gives both fathers and mothers the privilege of leaving a magnificent legacy through their children.

I've mentioned many benefits of having two parents in the home. Mainly because it takes an extraordinary effort to parent alone. Being an intentional parent is not for the faint at heart. I want you to know that you are truly amazing. I want you to see that you had other choices. By loving your children, hanging in there, and caring for them, you made a wise choice; especially when abandonment is an option. If you are unsure how to begin to be more intentional in your parenting or have completely dropped the ball with your children, you can make strides to turn things around. It will be one of your best decisions for yourself and your children.

Legacy is anything handed down from the past, but the legacy you want to leave your children is far more than that. You are leaving your children a legacy that is an inheritance of tangible and intangible possessions. You can't leave a legacy if you are only concerned about your pleasure and happiness. Making children happy is not the end game either. In an article about family legacies by J. Otis Ledbetter and Kurt Bruner, they state, "No matter who we are, where we live, or what our goals may be, we will all have one thing in common: a heritage. That is, a social, emotional, and spiritual legacy passed on from parent to child. Every one of us is passed a heritage, lives out a heritage, and gives a heritage to our family. It's not an option. Parents always pass to their children a legacy… good, bad, or some of both."[1]

The Gift of Forgiveness

While writing this book, Cortez found his dad through a relative on social media. He didn't even tell me until he had already contacted his dad. I was stunned and flooded with emotions. One sentiment was fear. He had not seen or spoken to his father in several years, and my concern was that his dad might reject him again.

Along with my initial fear of him being rejected was the fear of loss of control. Cortez was no longer a five-year-old who needed me to shield him, guide the relationship, and hug him tightly to comfort him. He was a young man seeking answers, and although I was still responsible for protecting him, it was a very different type of protection. At sixteen, my job was to ensure that his father was not in a place in his life where he would do something to cause our son harm. After I spoke with my son about his encounter, my last reaction was a delight. Cortez shared details about their conversation and the new things he learned about his dad. Cortez had no idea how I felt hearing specific things I knew I would question his dad about once I spoke with him. As he talked, I realized that Cortez showed great courage and maturity by contacting his dad. My mother used to call him a mini-me because he likes to ask bold questions. I was proud of him and how he handled himself.

I watched him go through the reconciliation process with his father, and it wasn't all good, but he got to know his father for himself and formed his own opinions about their relationship. It has been more than a year since he has been back in his life. It's not a picture-perfect situation, and it hasn't been stress-free, but it brings me joy to know that my son is operating within one of the biggest lessons I've taught him. That lesson is always to leave forgiveness on the table. Cortez forgiving his father wasn't an automatic entry for his father to come back into his life or a way of pretending that his dad didn't abandon him. Forgiveness was a gift so that Cortez could let go of the anger and the hurt to be reconciled with his dad.

Where did I fit in all of this? I positioned myself in the middle, supporting my son's decision in a responsible and healthy way. I wish I could tell you that it was a breeze. I'm a type-A personality, and I internalize things. I had to force myself to have an "it's not about me" mindset until it sank deep into my heart. It had nothing to do with me thinking about what his dad did to me all those years ago. I still felt a tinge of resentment and anger about what he had done to our son, and I wanted to protect him from that pain. I put those concerns aside because I did not want to influence Cortez's opinion of him negatively. I asked his dad straightforward questions about his situation and intentions. I remained skeptical until he was willing to show that he would put forth the effort. For Cortez's sake, I chose to compromise on making provisions for him to see his dad. I listened when he talked with me about his dad, I challenged him on his expectations for his dad, and I backed off when he wanted to work through his emotions.

To be honest, Cortez did what most children eventually do. They look for answers about who they are. Whether or not your children can articulate it, a child's desire to know an absent father or mother is a reality. I don't know how things will turn out with Cortez and his dad. It takes time and commitment to build trust. My love and responsibility for him is not dependent on his dad's involvement. If he never reconnected with his dad, I am still responsible for handing down a positive legacy that affirms him to pass down to his children.

In the *Diary of a Single Mother*, Elder Bernice King gave tribute to her mother, Coretta Scott King, who became a single mom of four after the assassination of Dr. Martin Luther King. In her own words, "She spent the first years after my father's assassination figuring out not what to do, but how to do it, and that was she knew she wanted to carry on his legacy, but now she had to figure out how do I do this in light of the fact that I have these four kids. How am I going to make sure that their stability is not interrupted?"[2] When I read those words from Elder King about her mom, I see that Coretta Scott King had to be thinking, "It's not about me."

It Takes Two

My fearless belief is that every child deserves a loving father and mother. My confidence in that statement is the driving force behind this book, and I want to touch on something near and dear to my heart: co-parenting. I talked about it earlier, but it does demand some special attention.

Even if you have never been married or if you are divorced, co-parenting well is one of the best gifts you can give your children if you are not going to be together. It is an entirely selfless act to do what is in the best interest of your children. Depending on the circumstance, co-parenting may not always be possible, but if you can create a successful co-parenting relationship, there are significant benefits for your children. Having both parents working together to provide love, understanding, and support is powerful. It gives children stability, security, and closeness with both parents, which is a win/win situation. A family legacy, where children can bring together traditions and values from both dad and mom, can surpass the negative inheritance that can come from feuding parents.

While I was married to Cortez's dad, I had a good relationship with Cortez's older brother's mother. Both families worked together to determine the dynamics of mixing well in blended families. It wasn't always easy, but we all shared something in common, we wanted what was in the best interest of our sons. We would coordinate as many activities as possible so that Cortez and his brother shared in each other's major life events, such as birthdays, holidays, family outings, and school events. We prioritized successful co-parenting so our children would reap the benefits. Again, it is all about following that "it's not about me" mindset.

Co-parenting is about sharing the duties of parenting. Sharing parental duties gives children a chance to experience the benefits of the parent's agreeing that the love for their children is more important than anything else. The inability to co-parent shouldn't stem from making the other person pay for not being in a relationship with you or moving on with someone else. While getting child support from a non-custodial parent should be a requirement, it should not be a precondition for someone to see their child. It is human nature to respond more to quality of time over wasteful quantity of time or material things. Seeing parents develop a way of working together and being respectful to one another will contribute to the legacy you leave your children.

The Legacy of Love

I began this book by sharing my testimony of how I became a single parent. My son was born out of wedlock. I married and then divorced his father. This was by no means an account of a fairy-tale love story where the princess and prince charming live happily ever after. Still, through our son, it is a genuine narrative of my first experience of knowing how to give unconditional love.

My love for my son is indescribable. When he was born, I suffered from undiagnosed post-partum depression. I felt disconnected, sad, and empty about everything and everyone except for my little guy. When I looked past what seemed to be an endless cycle of crying, poop, spit-up, and constant attention, all I saw and felt was my love for him. I wanted him to feel how much I loved him and show him he could count on me.

My love for him now is even stronger. Yes, without hesitation, I can still say that as we navigated through the ups and downs of his teenage years.

My memories of growing up without a father make me think of my grandmother, who showered me with unconditional love and made me feel like I was her only grandchild, even though she had many. She always made me feel special, and to this day, I've never seen anyone display the type of compassion for others that she expressed. I am fanatical about encouraging other parents because of my grandmother's demonstrative acts of love toward others. She had no money or material things to give, but she had a kind-heartedness that she gave wholeheartedly. Her love towards me was the most remarkable display of love ever shown to me in human form, and I pour that into my son because her legacy lives in me. I did not know a cherished love from my mother until I was an adult. I would not have known how to love my son and return love to my mother if it was not for my grandmother.

I asked Cortez to think about ways I've shown my love for him and share a memory that stood out. He quickly recalled a memory when he was about thirteen years old. One day when it was bitterly cold outside, he and a friend cut through a field to get home, and he slipped on some ice and fell in a puddle of water. When he arrived home, he was in tears from being so cold. He remembers walking in the door and me dropping everything I was doing to take care of him. He couldn't feel his legs or toes, and he was scared. He said, "Mom, you took care of me. You got me out of the wet clothes, wrapped me up, and got me in front of the fireplace fast. You got hand and toe warmers and rubbed different parts of my body until I got warm. You kept telling me everything would be okay and then made me some hot chocolate. I remembered that day because earlier you told me you had some important work to handle. You didn't care about that; you only cared about me."

My recollection of that day was panic because I contemplated getting him to the hospital. I didn't know how long he had been exposed to the cold air. His pants and socks were stiff, and I could barely get them off. My mind was racing, wondering if he had frostbite and if it was severe that he could lose an extremity. It was a gut instinct to care for him the way I did, but I was nervous. He made the emotional connection of that being a time when he felt loved by me, and that memory will be part of my legacy that will live on with him years down the line when I'm gone.

You may parent alone, but as you experience these special moments with your children, they may not say it enough, but they remember your sacrifices and love.

~SINGLE PARENT 101~
Parenting With Love

- *What does love look like for you as a single parent?*

   As a single parent, you can develop an amazing and unique bond with your children. You have the extraordinary privilege of showing them that love requires putting aside your needs to meet someone else's needs. That lesson can be taught in any home, but you demonstrate this act of love naturally when you are the one that they depend on for care and support.

- *How can you embrace an "it's not about me" mindset?*

   "It's not about me" doesn't mean you completely ignore your needs. You must give more of yourself and do that unselfishly and without regret. Your thoughts and actions must align with your heart. Your children need to know and feel loved by you and recognizing that they have a void can help you determine how to give of yourself in a healthy way that will be encouraging.

- *What is the legacy you want to leave?*

   I didn't want Cortez only to be influenced by my narrow view of life. I realized that what I did throughout his childhood would affect his tomorrow. Through my faith and being intentional in my parenting, I found that I could be the kind I mother I desired and instill values that could inspire Cortez to live out his purpose.

- *How do you see your positive impact?*

Turn the tables on the adverse effects of being a single parent. Let your choices be motivated by love, and never minimize how important you are to your children. You can create a home that infuses a strong sense of family values and promotes the kind of love that will influence the next generation.

CHAPTER NINE

Life Happens

*"Raising your child well is hard.
But learning to let them go out into the world and
prove that you did your job right is even tougher."*
– J. Craine

Letting your child "go out into the world," for all intents and purposes, typically means when your child becomes an adult. Many people compare this phase of parenting to how adult birds throw their babies out of their nests. As you push your son or daughter out of the imaginary nest into adulthood, you expect them to fly and soar high. There are several reasons why adult birds throw babies out of their nests. One well-known reason is that babies thrown from the nest instinctively start flapping their wings, trying to fly. Like children, baby birds go through growth-related stages before they are nudged out of the nest. Each stage is essential for the baby bird's development, and parents must provide the necessary care to ensure their young ones survive. It's easy to understand why this analogy for parenting is so popular. With it comes the expectation that you have thoroughly prepared your child to navigate life successfully. Fortunately for us, in most cases, our children get to spend many years under our supervision before they enter adulthood. But what, if anything, can we do to give them a chance to survive and thrive?

"These are the 'things' that change boys to men" is a line from the 1988 "Boys to Men" song by the R&B group New Edition.[1] A few of those 'things' they spoke about in the song are to keep growing, learning, and maturing even when you don't know it's happening. I find wisdom in reflecting on those lyrics because those 'things' are necessary regardless of gender, age, background, or life circumstances. Helping our children grow, learn, and mature never ends. As we help them through the various stages of life, doing our jobs right as parents, in general, will always come from a biased perspective. That bias can be positive or negative and will naturally be one-sided as a single parent. If you've been the only or primary parent raising your child, no matter how many pats on the back you get or judgments you receive from others, you are still inclined to gauge your success by your standards. With two parents, a collaborative effort should take place to determine right and wrong choices for your child. Both parents have their standards but have an opportunity to evaluate their decisions against another person's reasoning. When life gets hard, due to either something that happens to your child directly or to you that directly impacts your child, how do you help them grow, learn, and mature?

Three months after publishing the first edition of this book, my son's father died. Cortez was sixteen at the time, and whatever wisdom I thought I had as a parent at that point went out the window. As I walked to his room early in the morning to tell him that his father died, I recalled recently seeing him in the kitchen and telling him that when he made a particular face, he looked just like his dad. He was full of hope when he saw his father in the hospital the day before he died. Hearing the news was devastating for him, and I was brokenhearted for him as he cried in my arms. I had known his dad since I was fifteen years old, and although we divorced, I had no regrets for trying to be a family for our son. The bottom didn't just fall out of my son's life; it shattered his world. I went from being a single mother of an only child due to divorce to learning to be a single mother to my son through losing his father. I had to learn what to do as a parent to support him. Although I had tons of support and resources, I practically fumbled and stumbled through that season of life. At times I had to drag him as a soldier wounded in combat to get him to safety because he could not walk on his own and was too heavy to carry. I refused to stand by and watch him die mentally and emotionally from that loss and other trauma he had experienced earlier. My son's father's death was one of several major life-changing events we experienced that year. As the saying goes, "Life happens, when you least expect it".[2]

Cortez was depressed, his grades dropped, he began to isolate himself, and he eventually tried marijuana for the first time during his time of grief. All of my efforts to reach him failed. I'm a fixer and being unable to fix my son's pain brought me pain. Knowing that Cortez would never have the chance to have the relationship with his father that he desired made me think about all of the life events that his father previously missed. Although his father was absent most of his life, my son still had hope of what could be, and now that aspiration was taken away. With the help of my village, counseling, support from the staff at his high school, and, quite honestly, prayer, he made it through the tough time.

The Good, The Bad, The Ugly

If I had to rate if being raised by a single parent was good or bad, it depends on which season of life you are evaluating and if I believe my life results accurately indicate that my life is successful. My adult life appears to back up the assumption that things turned out well. By all accounts, I am living the illusion of the American dream. I'm married, have a beautiful family, make an honest living, and have made no glaring choices that have left me so damaged by my upbringing that I couldn't overcome. Up until the age of eighteen, I considered myself low maintenance. I had a few challenges adjusting to the move from Illinois to Missouri when I was in the 8th grade, but for the most part, I stayed out of trouble, got good grades, and graduated from high school seemingly unscarred.

Everyone expected that I would do well in life, and my accomplishments support that assertion. I use words like "seemingly" and "appear" because I was broken underneath the well-put-together little girl who grew up to be a very independent, self-sufficient woman. I can't say with certainty that my mother intentionally filled the gap with positive male role models in my father's absence. Still, I can confidently say that consistently having a caring male's love, affirmation, and guidance would have positively affected my life. My father was a lifelong drug addict and could not reciprocate emotions nor function in healthy relationships. Whether he had been in the home or fulfilled the bare minimum of being present, it doesn't seem like it would have made much of a difference. It could have even been detrimental to my life. So, the question remains, did I need both parents? Does it matter if I turned out "all right?" Yes, it does matter, and no, it doesn't. Wait, what? Stay with me; let me explain.

If you can recall, in chapter two, I stated that, "Successful parenting is not defined by how your children turn out. It is defined by how you care for them along the way." This principle is true in both single-parent and two-parent homes. The significance of single-parent homes is that you are guaranteed to work overtime to compensate for the absent parent. Intentionally filling the gap does not secure perfect or even good outcomes. Still, it matters because it gives you a better chance to lower the risks of your child developing negative behaviors and making dangerous choices more likely to be made by children brought up only by a single parent. I only say it doesn't matter because, despite our upbringing, we can rise above any statistics and defy the odds. With the complexity of the concept of nature versus nurture and how we process our experiences, there is a chance that we can be unaffected or minimally impacted in the long run by events that would otherwise support that our lives are simply the cause and effect of our upbringing. However, our children's well-being isn't a game of Russian Roulette to be left up to chance alone. As a single parent, intentional parenting that addresses some gaps of having an absent parent can make a difference.

Small Victories Win the War

Throughout this book, I have connected with you on so many levels. Given that we have different backgrounds and experiences, love for our children is the common factor that brings us to a place of agreement. Our love for our children encourages us to push through every obstacle we've discussed. Sometimes you must work twice as hard to give your children a chance to rise above the statistics of being raised by one parent. Remember that stability is not defined just by family structure. You overcome the odds one decision at a time and cultivate love with your children so they will walk in that same love as they enter the world and begin building their lives. You are responsible for providing a reliable and safe home, consistent emotional and social support, and teaching healthy values to help your children develop and carry out that legacy for future generations. The legacy of intangible possessions you leave your children, above all other things, should be

LOVE. Your work is the same as it is for children who are raised by a dad and mom. You are to raise your children in a way that will help them develop into loving, healthy, responsible, and effective adults who will positively impact this world.

I am proud to stand with you and tell you that YOU CAN DO IT.

~SINGLE PARENT 101~
Expecting the Unexpected

- *How can you learn to spill love into your children at every phase of life?*

    From infancy to when they become adults, your love will be the most reliable gift you can give your children. I'm not just discussing the emotion of love but also the decisions that demonstrate love. Take the time to understand the ever-changing needs of your children. Learn how to nurture and not hinder their growth and development.

- *What are your greatest fears when it comes to parenting?*

    It's not uncommon to have concerns about unpredictable circumstances in parenting. Being a single parent can add to those fears when you don't have trust that the other parent will have your back. Acknowledge your fears. Come to terms with the reality that many of the things you fear are out of your control, and few, if any, of your fears come to fruition.

- *Who can you depend on during difficult seasons of parenting?*

    Watching your children go through painful experiences or struggle through challenging times can be gut-wrenching. Going through it alone is hard. It is good to have someone in your life who can provide a listening ear, share words of encouragement, or offer practical solutions. Having others in your corner who love your child and care about you is an invaluable support system.

- *How can you continue to help your children keep growing, learning, and maturing through the ups and downs of life?*

As early as they understand the message, teach your children that life is a journey. Through each stage of life, you should be growing, learning, and maturing along with them. Adjust to meet their physical, cognitive, emotional, and social needs. When you are ready to nudge them out of the nest, watch them flap their wings like crazy to fly.

NOTES

Introduction
1. *Forrest Gump*, directed by Robert Zemeckis (1994; United States: Paramount Pictures), DVD.
2. Focus on the Family, *The Family Project: A Divine Reflection*, United States: Pine Creek Entertainment, (2014.)

Chapter 1. We Are Family
1. *Family*, (1913), In *Merriam Webster*. Retrieved from http://www.webster-dictionary.org/definition/family.
2. *Family*, (2016), In *Dictionary.com*. Retrieved from http://www.dictionary.com/browse/family.

Chapter 2. The Heart of the Matter
1. Kevin Durant, "Full MVP Award Ceremony Speech," (Filmed May 7, 2014, Video File). Retrieved from https://www.youtube.com/watch?v=wac3CtzcLO4.
2. Mike Murdock, "2 Minute Wisdom with Dr. Mike Murdock," (June 5, 2017). Retrieved from https://youtu.be/qYX6BeF80qo.

3. Lee, De. *Single Mother Statistics.* (August 22, 2017). Retrieved from https://singlemotherguide.com/single-mother-statistics/.
4. Jonathan Vespa, Jamie M. Lewis, and Rose M. Kreider, "America's Families Families and Living Arrangements: 2012, *U.S. Census Bureau,* (August 2013). Retrieved from chrome-https://post.ca.gov/portals/0/post_docs/publications/Building%20a%20Career%20Pipeline%20Documents/safe_harbor.pdf
5. Lewis, J., Vespa, J. (U.S. Census Bureau, 2009-2011 American Community Surveys, 2012 Condition of Children in Orange County, America's Families and Living Arrangements. Retrieved from chrome-https://post.ca.gov/portals/0/post_docs/publications/Building%20a%20Career%20Pipeline%20Documents/safe_harbor.pdf
6. *The Karate Kid,* Directed by John G. Avildsen, (1984, United States: Columbia Pictures,) DVD.

Chapter 3. The Best Things in Life are Free
1. J. Kirby, *Single Parent Families in Poverty.* Retrieved from http://www3.uakron.edu/schulze/401/readings/singleparfam.htm
2. G. Livingston, *The Rise of Single Fathers.* (July 2, 2013). Retrieved from http://www.pewsocialtrends.org/2013/07/02/the-rise-of-single-fathers/
3. B. Eliiot, *Chris Gardner: A Determined Father.* Retrieved from http://www1.cbn.com/movies/chris-gardner-determined-father

Chapter 5. Flying Solo
1. Tony Fonte, telephone interview to author, May 20, 2017.

Chapter 6. Count the Cost
1. B. Schmitt, *Sticky Situations II*, Tyndale House Publishers (Aug 1, 2001).
2. Mike Murdock, "2 Minute Wisdom with Dr. Mike Murdock," (June 5, 2017.) Retrieved from https://youtu.be/qYX6BeF80qo.

Chapter 7. Do As I Say, Not As I Do
1. Creating a Stable Home for our Kids (2022). Solo Parent. Retrieved from https://soloparent.org/blog/2022/04/10/creating-a-stable-home-for-our-kids
2. Heather Lonczak. (May 8, 2019) Title. PositivePsychology.com Retrieved from https://positivepsychology.com/positive-parenting/
3. First Things First (2023). Retrieved from https://www.firstthingsfirst.org/early-childhood-matters/brain-development/#:~:text=At%20birth%2C%20the%20average%20baby's,center%20of%20the%20human%20body.
4. S. Covey, *The 7 Habits of Highly Successful People,* New York City: NY Free Press, (1989).

Chapter 8. It's Not About Me
1. Picdottv. *The Diary of a Single Mother: Mrs. Coretta Scott King.* (Oct. 5, 2010, Video File). Retrieved from https://www.youtube.com/watch?v=QM3QvypbWh0

Chapter 9. Life Happens
1. J. Harris and T. Lewis, "New Edition - Lyrics to Boys to Men," *Heart Break Album,* MCA, (Jun. 20, 1988). Retrieved from https://www.discogs.com/master/149858-New-Edition-Heart-Break
2. Jodi Picoult, "Life Happens, When You Least Expect It."

ABOUT THE AUTHOR

LATARISS PAYNE is a talented writer, gifted speaker, and visionary who loves to inspire people to make dynamic decisions that push them forward to overcome adversity. She spent much of her career in the corporate sector as an IT Leader at a Fortune 500 Financial Services firm. She graduated from Webster University, where she received her Master's Degree in IT Management, and she has a certification in Biblical Counseling.

Latariss is married to her husband, Calvin. She was a single mother to her son until he reached adulthood and now has a family of four children and two grandchildren. She encourages and empowers other single parents through her book and public speaking. Latariss and her message bring thought-provoking, practical and inspiring insights for all single parents and their most important gift of raising responsible, caring children.

Latariss firmly believes in having a work-life balance and has developed a desire to help women navigate the challenges of pursuing their dreams while caring for their families. She combines her savvy experience in leadership and personal development and her love for the family to help others discover joy and fulfillment in their personal and professional lives.

To contact the author, email info@pathsetters.com. To find out more about Latariss, visit www.pathsetters.com.

www.ingramcontent.com/pod-product-compliance
Lightning Source LLC
Chambersburg PA
CBHW070431010526
44118CB00014B/2000